920

W9-BAI-109

Civil Rights Childhood

Civil Rights Childhood

Jordana Y. Shakoor

University Press of Mississippi
Jackson

http://www.upress.state.ms.us

02 01 00 99   4 3 2 1

The paper in this book meets the guidelines for permanence and durability
of the Committee on Production Guidelines for Book Longevity of
the Council on Library Resources.

Library of Congress Cataloging-in-Publication Data

Shakoor, Jordana Y., 1956–
Civil rights childhood / Jordana Y. Shakoor.
p.   cm.
ISBN 1-57806-192-X (cloth : alk. paper)
1. Shakoor, Jordana Y., 1956–   —Childhood and youth.   2. Jordan,
Andrew L., d. 1991.   3. Afro-Americans—Biography.   4. Fathers—
United States—Biography.   5. Daughters—United States—Biography.
6. Afro-Americans—Civil rights—Mississippi—Greenwood—
History—20th century.   7. Civil rights movements—Mississippi—
Greenwood—History—20th century.   8. Jordan family.   9. Greenwood
(Miss.)—Biography.   I. Title.
E185 96.S42   1999
973'.0496073'0092—dc21
[b]
99-12826
CIP

British Library Cataloging-in-Publication Data available

Contents

Memories

His smile reminds me of golden leaves
Sweet potatoes
Stories of a Mississippi boyhood
Books about black people
Pigtails braided by big clumsy hands
Sitting on his lap
Listening to his wisdom
Looking into his eyes
So much was there for me
My first love
My daddy

Preface

When I was a child, I said proudly to anyone who would listen, "My daddy is a schoolteacher." There were few black professionals at that time in Mississippi, so for someone to become a schoolteacher was a great achievement; many blacks were relegated to picking cotton or driving tractors on plantations. Throughout his life, my father inspired students, colleagues, and many others to achieve their goals by describing to them the tremendous obstacles he had had to overcome in order to fulfill his own dreams.

The story in this book is told in two voices, my father's and my own. My father's words, taken from the journals that he kept for a number of years, appear in italics. When Daddy died in 1991, I recovered two rubber-banded, bound notebooks from a nightstand next to his side of the bed. I knew they were there, because I had first read them when I was twelve years old. I took them home for safekeeping. Two years ago when I was missing him, I read them again.

In the notebooks, my father recounts what it was like to be a black boy in the cotton fields of Mississippi. I read about his hopes and his dream of becoming a schoolteacher even though he came from a family of dirt-poor Negro sharecroppers. Through his words, I relived his activism in the civil rights movement in Greenwood, Mississippi. I felt his pain and frustration with the racist society that killed Medgar Evers. I understood his feelings of cowardliness and his initial reluctance to take a stand for fear of jeopardizing the well-being of his family.

Yet there was much that Daddy didn't write, and that is why I decided to intertwine our stories in an effort to fill in the gaps, to give an account that would encompass his whole life. I have also endeavored to describe the major events that shaped the lives of the Jordan family. In doing so, I celebrate the lives of many other African American families.

These accounts were written for my parents and for the thousands of blacks who died before they could vote in a country that they had given their sweat and blood so humbly to build. And it is for my wife, five daughters, and unborn generations, so they will know that democracy is only a word without meaning, and shall forever be, until the hearts and souls of men and women everywhere are willing to accept people of all races on the basis of their goodness and not their pigmentation.

Civil Rights Childhood

"Why do you say 'Yes, Suh' to him, Papa?" I asked.
"I'm supposed to, Son," he replied as he walked on ahead.

Son of Mississippi Sharecroppers

Andrew L. Jordan, my father, was the fourth of five seedlings that sprang from the union of Cleveland and Elizabeth Jordan. Daddy was born in the land of the Mississippi River, which snakes through a rich Delta soil. He was mired in the ugliness of a southern philosophy according to which white skin was supreme and black skin inferior. He languished in a land of lily-white magnolias where for centuries blacks had had no freedom. It was a mesmerizing place that nourished the roots of people who endured years of injustice. My family was born in the most racist state in the union.

The Charles Whitington plantation in Rising Sun County, where Daddy was raised, is right outside Greenwood, Mississippi. The little town of Greenwood is located in Leflore County, which was named after a French/Choctaw Indian chieftain named Greenwood Leflore. By the 1900s, Greenwood had become an important Delta town known for its long-staple cotton market. The county's population was almost two-thirds Negro and poor. The Jordan family was among them.

In 1937, Daddy was a six-year-old colored boy. Large for his age, he was already struggling to pull more than he weighed through the fields of King Cotton. One hot sweaty day, he innocently asked his father why he had answered "yes, sir" to a white boy not older than about thirteen, a nasty-tempered kid, who didn't know better than to wipe snot on the sleeves of his ragged blue shirt. The reply my grandfather gave him — "I'm supposed to, Son" — only intensified the negative self-image that had been growing in my father.

Papa had plowed almost five rows of cotton in the ninety-degree weather. You could see the heat waves dancing in space, and occasionally a wisp of wind would twist itself from the heated dust, blowing the sweaty mule smell right into my nose.

I could tell very easily that it was getting close to lunchtime, even though we had no watch from which to tell time. The old mule that Papa had named Old Gray had begun to disobey him.

"Well, Son, it's about time to take Old Gray to the barn to be fed," Papa said as he brought the mule to a halt. Then he walked behind Old Gray and unhooked him from the plow. I started to help.

"No, Son, your Papa will do it; you might get hurt," he added softly as he patted my eager hands away.

My father and I talked very little while en route to the barn. The heat seemed to have absorbed all the vigor from him. But Old Gray had to be fed and watered first. That was part of the plantation rule. While Old Gray was eating and kicking up his heels, Papa and I sat in the quiet shade of the big white barn. He offered me some water from the tin bucket I had brought for him to quench his thirst. For our lunch, we ate a couple ears of corn apiece.

Then Papa rested against the barn wall. Routinely he took out his little Old Testament Bible from his sweaty overall pocket and read aloud a passage or two. As he read the Bible, I could see signs of fatigue in his eyes, but the determination to read out-weighed his exhaustion. He read silently for about a half-hour, then the whistle blew. It was one o'clock. Slowly Papa rose from the shady corner, picking up the bridle as he attempted to elevate his tired body to an upright position. Only he found he was almost too weak to stand. When he had steadied himself, we walked out to the big white barn gate. He rested his heavy hand on my little boy shoulder. Almost immediately Old Gray saw him coming and began circling around the other mules in an effort to conceal his identity. After chasing the mule for at least ten minutes, Papa was able to subdue him. Once old Gray was cornered, he would surrender rather easily. But always he would give Papa a chase.

Papa had returned to the field ready to resume work, when his bossman's son came up on horseback.

"Boy, did you take Old Gray to the barn?" He asked Papa this while sitting tall on a big reddish-brown horse.

"Yes, Suh, Mr. Charles, Old Gray done eat," my father answered him with a tired voice as sweat dropped musically down his back, retracing the sweaty streaked lines of his blue work shirt.

"Is that boy any good, Cleve?" Young Mr. Charles had made reference to me.

"Yes, Suh, he a fine boy, Boss," my father answered to him.

The bossman's son looked at me as though he was thinking, "I'll work the hell out of him in a few years." I looked only at Papa, who was hitching Old Gray back up to the plow. I didn't like that white boy.

My father, however, learned to be thankful for his life in those days of growing up in Mississippi with his brothers. Clevester, the oldest, was the handsome one who escaped Jim Crow after World War II. Will was considered the "crazy" brother, having once been shipped to a mental hospital in Jackson for shock treatment because he had dared to slap a white man four times, each blow coming after the man got up off the ground and called him "nigger." My father came to realize that, even though his stomach was growling with emptiness while he and his brothers slept in a crowded bed, at least all of them were there and not hanging by the noose of a rope that was too short. Along with his younger brother, David, and his sister, Viola, he learned that the length of a black man's life in Mississippi was at the whim of a white man.

For years, Daddy witnessed his father, a medium-built, dark-skinned, Bible scripture-spouting man, and then his older brothers sharecrop land they didn't own and would never own. Before too long, he found himself standing in a sea of cotton.

At seven years old, Daddy was required to labor in the fields, and he began to feel stagnated by the endless acres of cotton. His full lips would protrude with indignation, and his dark, brooding eyes would repeatedly question the manhood of black fathers who were turned into stuttering idiots by redneck overseers barely able to read a newspaper.

The fact that his family remained so poor perplexed my father. It didn't make sense to him when his father, whose back ached at the beginning of the day and who by nightfall would be bent over in painful contortions, worked so hard. He soon learned that carrying the cross of racism was taking a toll on his father's body and his mother's, too, as it had across the generations, and that the legacy of being a sharecropper was probably the only inheritance his father would leave the children.

When Daddy was a boy, of course, he didn't just work in the cotton fields and learn to resent white folks. He and his siblings had many wonderful childhood experiences. The members of their close-knit family were teasing characters who loved to joke with one another. They would talk for hours around the dinner table or compete with the crickets out on the porch under a blanket of stars.

On many evenings, colored neighbors with children in tow would seek their company, and, on holidays, would share a pot-luck dinner. And yearly the Jordan family would plant a big vegetable garden, then harvest from it as they needed to, in between times of gathering the cotton. Surplus from the garden would be shared with half-hungry and grateful neighbors.

The family would walk to church together on Sundays, because they had no other way of getting there. On the dirt road, they would meet other colored folks who needed some good gospel as well. They could have stayed home; Granddaddy Jordan knew the Bible backwards and forwards, and he could preach just as well as any man of God. Besides, he gave a sermon every day, rain or shine, through good times as well as bad.

After supper Daddy and a brother or two would walk for a couple of miles up the road to play with the other colored children, who lived in shacks like their own. The boys would fish until they got tired of it or had caught all that their families could eat; then, if it was hot enough, they would jump into the water and swim, laugh, and clown around. On summer afternoons, they would run races barefooted, rolling old tires along the dirt road. Their hands would beat the tires, "splaat, splaat," and clay-like dust would fly into their faces and hair, making muddy streaks across their shirtless bodies. By the end of the day they would be much too dirty to enter the house. Then Grandmama Jordan would insist that Daddy and his brothers take a hot bath outside in the big tin tub with Palmolive soap. They would have to be quick about their bathing as they fought the mosquitoes.

During the hunting season, Daddy, his brothers, and their father hunted with sticks that had rocks tied to the ends. With these weapons they knocked silly or killed plenty of rabbits and pheasants. Wild rabbit in a bed of rice, smothered in gravy, with mustard greens and yams was one of Daddy's favorite meals.

Fall of that year was bad, and it was difficult to gather all that was planted. We barely were able to gather our corn and potatoes before winter. Many plantations weren't able to gather all the cotton. Lucky for us, we were always among those who finished because Papa was determined to maintain his reputation as a good working nigger who got his work done on time. We made twenty-five bales of cotton that year. A bale of cotton consists of thirteen hundred pounds with seeds included, depending upon what kind of cotton was being gathered. There are two types of cotton, short-staple and long-staple. If we used short-staple cotton it would only take 1,300 pounds, but if we were using long-staple, it would take 1,500 pounds of cotton to make a bale. Long-staple was more acceptable.

Usually after harvest, we would kill hogs; they were to substitute for our lack of money to buy food. From the hogs we got lard, crackling, and meat. There was no sense in expecting much money from the cotton we had made, because usually we would end up owing the white man anyway.

There was never a definite date set for settlement. However, we could usually expect it before Christmas, like two or three days before. This was done to keep the tenants from borrowing money for Christmas. Customarily around the middle of December black people would start hanging around the store hoping to overhear something about when the settlement date was going to be.

"Good morning, Brother Jordan," said an old friend of Papa's who happened to be passing the house one afternoon.

"Have you heard anything about when the man is gone settle?" He asked this while leaning on the picket fence.

"Jack, I ain't heard nothin'," replied my father in exasperation as he walked toward him. "I guess the bossman will settle with us colored people next week," he added.

Talk like that would go on for weeks until eventually something would happen. Sooner or later a Negro might be sitting around the plantation store, and overhear the man say when he was going to settle, or maybe the man would just come in and settle with him and tell him to spread the word among the other niggers that settlement would be the following day.

On Settlement Day the sharecroppers would get what the white man gave them without any questions asked and walk out pretending to be satisfied. If they showed any dissatisfaction, they were usually asked to move for fear they would spoil the rest of the niggers.

There was one Negro called J. T. who always got paid in one dollar bills and a lot of change money. He couldn't count money. To make him think that he had gotten a lot of money for his year's work, his bossman would pay him in that manner. Usually it would not be more than a hundred dollars.

My father received his settlement early one morning in December. He was among the first to get his money. I rode my bike up to the store in time to see a lot of sad faces. Papa's was one of those faces, and he was also bitter about his outcome. We had made twenty-five bales of cotton that year, but Papa had gotten only three hundred dollars for all the work we had done. There were others who had made more cotton then us and had not cleared a cent, and there were others who had made more and cleared similar amounts. One family had made forty-five bales of cotton and gathered all of it with their children half-eating. This family cleared only five hundred dollars. This was the Miller family. They would always make a little more money than the rest of the black people.

All week long my mother had sat around the house with my sister and brothers, waiting to learn what the year's work had earned for us. As I rode the bike that five of us children shared, I listened to my father talking to himself, as he walked from the plantation store, counting over and over the three hundred dollars he had received for all of our hard work. I heard him say, "It's better den nothin'. We den't get nothin' last year."

Apparently, after my father had thought over the fact that he had received some money, he felt that somehow he had progressed. Papa was now looking kind of relieved. He was even beginning to smile as he neared the house. I had never before had any money, but I was mad as hell because he had received such a small amount. Papa, on the other hand, seemed to have become satisfied as he walked along the dusty road, not saying a word to me, only talking to himself.

We were within a half-mile of the house when Mama spotted us and came hurriedly to meet us. She met us about half the distance with a big broad smile on her magnificent face.

"What did we get this year?" she asked with a fixed smile on her face, only to have it fade away with the anticipation of a long unfulfilled dream.

"Beth," Papa said, "we cleared three hundred dollars." He always called her Beth instead of Elizabeth.

Mama tried hard to be nice by pretending that she was pleased. But because she had been disappointed so many times before, it was impossible for her to conceal her true feelings. She called Papa "Cleve." Only before it had been with a subordinate demeanor because she always felt that it was the man's duty to front the hardships.

"Cleve . . . is that really all we got?"

Mama asked this with signs of tears accumulating in her dark troubled eyes. My father dropped his head as though he was less than a man, as though he hadn't lived up to the expectations of his family.

Lifting his head with inferiority, he said, "Yes Beth, we only got three hundred dollars for all that work."

My mother couldn't hold her tears any longer. They began to spill down her face, in spite of her previous attempts to keep them concealed from us.

"I'll not farm anymore, Cleve. I can make that much money doing anything," she solemnly proclaimed.

Mama then turned and walked back into our three-room shack — a home that seemed to engulf what little spirit and hope we had left. She would tell the rest of the family. Papa, looking helpless, walked away in the direction of the wood pile. He muttered under his breath, "The Lord will make a way."

Papa had great faith. Perhaps that is what kept him going and what kept us believing in him for so many years. My mother didn't farm anymore after that year. She did domestic work from that day on.

The next year came and went swiftly, leaving us and many like us with less than what the white man's dog could eat. We had no money. We had only aching bones from hard work over the summer, and from the fall and winter, that always found us gathering the white man's cotton for the white man's bank account.

There was one year—I believe Daddy was about ten years old—when the bossman must have earned a fortune.

When I walked into the house, Mama and Papa were sitting at the kitchen table counting money. They were happy, for it was a lot of money. It was more money than I had ever seen. And as far as I knew, it was more money than they had ever seen.

"Hi, Mama. Hi, Papa," I said pulling up a chair on the opposite side of the table. Both of them spoke to me without turning their heads the least bit from the pile of money. As he counted the last twenty-dollar bill, I heard Papa say, "Six hundred."

"How much did you count, Beth?" They were counting in separate piles.

Mama finished her pile and said, "I have four hundred twenty-five dollars, Cleve."

"We have cleared a thousand dollars and more," I said to myself, not realizing I had spoken loud enough for anyone to hear.

"Yes, Son, we did well this year." Papa was smiling with joy.

But Papa had deliberately chosen not to think about the forty-five bales of cotton we had made, and the two thousand dollars short of what we should have gotten. They originally had figured we should have cleared thirty-five hundred dollars after all expenses were paid to our part. By not borrowing any money that year and not using any extra rations, my parents had tried to make sure the bossman wouldn't be able to say expenses had eaten up the profits. But nobody ever got what he or she thought they should have gotten. Papa and Mama were pleased so I made myself pleased as well, and so did all of us.

Most of the sharecropping the Jordan family did was on the Charles Whitington plantation. When the planting and harvesting there were accomplished as scheduled or sooner, they were loaned to the Malouf plantation. Old Man Malouf was a descendent of Arabs, so he wasn't an acceptable part of the white supremacist social order either. Nevertheless, the Maloufs were and still are one of the wealthiest families in Mississippi. When my grandmother stopped laboring in the cotton fields, she went to work as a maid in their hotel in Greenwood.

Experiences like my grandparents' were echoed thousands of times throughout the South by other disenfranchised Negro sharecroppers. White sharecroppers were also cheated. Although they made considerably more than Negroes, they still did not receive what they actually earned while getting those red necks in the sweltering heat. Of course, as long as those running the system could keep poor whites believing that the reason they were not prosperous was because niggers worked like grub worms during a drought, then the landowners would be the ones to benefit. And the poor whites could take comfort in the fact that it was always possible to whip together a lynch mob.

I walked soundlessly to the corner of the shed in time to hear a Negro in a low muffled voice say, "The Ku Klux Klan killed him."

Fear and Discrimination

Long before I was born and cradled in the protective arms of my father, white children in Mississippi were being read fairy tales written by Hans Christian Andersen, Charles Perrault, and Beatrix Potter. Hearing how Hansel and Gretel, lost in the forest, came upon a wicked witch who wanted to eat them instead of the candy-and-cake-decorated house with which she had lured them, these children could feel especially loved and cared for, lying like delicious morsels in the safety of their four-poster beds. They could tremble with delight at their father's deliberate metamorphosis into Little Red Riding Hood's big bad wolf. Little white girls could easily imagine themselves as Snow White or Cinderella, while little white boys could envision themselves as the Prince Charming who would come to rescue the damsels in distress.

In contrast, colored children like my father living in the Land of Cotton did not grow up with fairy tales that made them shiver in delicious fright. Instead, they were told gruesome tales of slavery, prejudice, and injustice. And they knew the tales were true ones, because many colored children had witnessed the actual remnants of black men swinging from trees. Colored children feared angry mobs of white men (sometimes of women and children, too).

There was stillness in the air almost unnoticeable, yet a tense feeling that would dawn on a person who wasn't preoccupied. In sight of the woods that surrounded our tin-top house, I lay awake between three brothers who slept in the same bed when I heard a shot that sounded like a big cannon. I was about seven years old at the time. Perhaps it was about two o'clock in the morning. I then heard foot steps that aren't meant to be heard, but I heard them. They were almost to the front gate of our house or at least it seemed as though they were there.

I heard voices, too, and they were voices of white men. I was frightened now and began to scream. My mother spurted to the rally of my cry and snatched me from among my brothers who were not awakened by the sound of the shotgun. My mother was shaking as her hand covered my mouth, while she and Papa paced the floor in the darkness. They, too, had heard the sounds. Only they understood what it was all about, because they had lived through this kind of thing all their lives.

In her fear Mama forgot she had her hand over my mouth and nose. It wasn't until I began to gasp for air that she discovered she was causing me to suffocate. I was quieted, then she put me into bed between her and Papa. The sound of footsteps was gone, but the whirl of hand-cranked Model T motors was noisy against the still of the night. Then they pulled off, leaving the evidence of another injustice imposed on a black man.

It was as many times before when the white man had washed his hands, tightened his tie, and gone back into his community with a clean conscience, as though nothing had happened. Many times he would be the same white savage that had participated the night before.

The next day dawned and there was crying. The cries were from his parents, sisters, brothers, and friends. Gordon had been living alone in a house, in the left corner of his boss's yard. His body was on a cot where he had been sleeping. His head had been blown off with buckshots. No policemen were called. There was only his bossman, his parents, his relatives, and a few other Negroes frightened almost to death.

No questions were asked, because they knew there were no answers to be given. His parents worked for these people, some of the richest in Mississippi, and they knew all about the lynching. No white man would go into another white man's yard and murder a Negro without his consent, not even the police in Mississippi.

Gordon was buried. The terrible thing was over, until it happened to another Negro.

A hush stayed in the air, stale as it was with a human being's blood so freshly wasted. A Negro's blood which nobody gave a damn about. He had been killed not by the pointing of a finger by a white woman, which was oftentimes the case, but by a jealous Negro who happened to have skin as black as Gordon's. They hadn't caught the woman with Gordon, or Gordon with her, which is apparently the only reason she hadn't yelled rape. His parents continued to work for the bossman as though nothing had happened.

"That was the best thing to do," his mother would say when asked about the lynching of her son. The reason they didn't speak out was because they didn't have any protection. The law did not represent Negroes. Negroes could not go against a white man or take him to court and live afterwards. No judge would take a Negro's word against a white man's. So she pretended it hadn't happened the way it had. It was better to blame her son and let it die like all cases involving Negroes and whites, especially when the Negro is the victim of a white.

My parents had become conciliatory, too, as they walked around apparently thinking that the same thing might happen to one of their own sons. We had to pass that place every day going and coming from school, and each day as I passed that place it made me angry. Had it had been a *brother of mine I could not have accepted Gordon's murder as easily as his parents and the other black people seemed to by simply saying he was out of his place.*

I never felt that people with black skin had to be humble, or submissive to white people. As I grew older, I often thought about those who asked for police protection only to find out that the policeman was a member of the Ku Klux Klan.

Not long after the incident, I stayed outside with my younger brother, David, playing cars with sardine cans.

"I'll never let a white man beat me, if I ever get into trouble. I won't stop killing him until I'm dead."

I kept talking to myself as I played, not realizing that Papa had come out of the house and was standing behind me.

"Son, you must get that out of your system," he told me in a very concerned tone. "Do you want to get all of us killed?" he asked angrily.

"No," I answered respectfully. "But Papa..." I started to say something else, but he cut right in.

"No more talking, Son, okay?" He looked down at me sternly.

"Okay, Papa," I said reluctantly.

Papa knew too well how the Ku Klux Klan operated. He knew of whole families being killed because of what one black man did. He had taken me much more seriously, perhaps, than I was at the time. However, I found myself as I grew older echoing those very same words.

The tales of what could happen to black men, women, and children were not the kind that made colored children squeal to fatigued parents, "More, more! Tell us more." These stories were relayed to black children not for bedtime pleasure but as a way of cautioning them to be careful, to stay in their places and never sass a white man or woman. Negro kids who did not heed their parents' warnings found to their embarrassment that they could be whipped by storekeepers while their parents looked on helplessly.

When colored children like my father heard the horrible but factual tales, they understood that what their mothers, fathers, aunts, uncles, grandmothers, and grandfathers actually were telling them was that "if they come to get you, we cannot help you. We cannot safeguard you, child, if the white men in sheets come to get you, because we can't even protect ourselves."

At about ten years old, I knew quite a bit about the Ku Klux Klan. That was one of the first things I learned about. I learned to say "KKK" perhaps before I learned to say "Da Da," because that was the talk in the family. At a very young age I remember my parents telling us that the KKK had killed a Negro woman's husband because he was accused of raping a white woman. This had been pounded into my head from as early as I can remember. Mama said that the lady was in the family way at the time of her husband's death. This man was tarred, staked down and burned while hundreds of white men and women stood watching.

After the flames had unjustly snuffed out his life, she said one white man with hatred dripping from his lips emerged from the crowd and shouted, "His woman is carrying a nigger bastard. Let's destroy the last damn seed of the SOB." She said all the whites in the mob had rallied to the call of the Klansmen, and at least twenty men had gone into the Negro woman's house and pulled her out by her heels. They then tied her to a pole with plow lines and ripped her grease soap dress from her body and made jokes as she stood there helplessly naked, unable to move anything except her head.

Mama said that then one of the Klansmen walked from behind the mob with a dagger in his hand. The crowd was quiet now. She said you could hear a pin fall. Mama said a Negro had witnessed it all, by peeping between his fingers behind a bush that scarcely concealed their evil deed.

The dagger cut into the Negro woman's belly, and she made one terrible groan, then flopped loosely hanging by her hands. The Klansman then stuck his hand into her and pulled out the unborn child and said, "This is the seed of the SOB." Then he threw it down beside its dead father's cremated body. Next a beast of a man who was smiling from ear to ear brought his big foot down and deformed what was a living human being. My Mama said, with tears rolling down her Indian-red cheeks, "When it was all over, he said the lynch mob walked away as though they had rid the world of one more evil."

Having heard this story from my parents, who heard it from their parents, and other people who knew it to be true, I had good knowledge of the Ku Klux Klan's tactics.

When little colored children like my father came up to size and could be taken seriously by whites, they were taught a black version of Emily Post's social decorum, a set of rules which might be called "How to Survive in the Racist State of Mississippi and Live to Tell About It." For instance, they were instructed not to look white folks who were speaking to them in the eye, because it might seem disrespectful. They learned not to stand too close to whites, who might think they were a threat. They knew that even if they were next in line, they should step aside and allow a white person to be waited on first. And they were taught to move off the sidewalk — even into the mud — to let a white person pass.

They were instructed always to say "yes, sir" and "yes, ma'am," even if the white person was younger than they were. They learned that if an individual had white skin or seemed to be passing for white, they should take no chances but keep their heads bowed and be respectful. If a white person was wrong, they knew never to point it out, because colored folks weren't supposed to be as intelligent as whites. They were taught to concede their seat when asked by a white, even if it was at the back of the bus, train, or trolley, where blacks were required to sit.

They were to use water fountains and rest rooms indicated by signs that said "colored only." If they couldn't find such a rest room, they had to use the bushes out beside the road or a Mason jar that was placed under the car seat for such emergencies.

Negro children were told that there were some really good white folks in Mississippi; they were even told who some of these individuals were and what kindnesses they had demonstrated. But, for the most part, they were taught to be wary of all white people, who stuck together. No white man had ever been convicted in a Mississippi court of law for maiming or killing a Negro.

Most important, when Negro boys like my father came into puberty, they were instructed to avoid white women and girls. They were told not to gaze at a woman directly even if she was looking at them, and that whistling or smiling at one would be an act of absolute stupidity that would amount to willingly placing their fool heads through the noose of a white man's rope.

Colored children might not be given all of these instructions literally; they also learned how to behave around whites by observing their parents. When they asked why, as my father did, they were told that this was how Negroes were supposed to behave. And it was strongly suggested that they act accordingly if they wanted to have a long life in Mississippi. Simply put, it was a matter of survival.

One day I was riding with a black man named Kent Smith when he tried to pass a white man in his car. The white man pulled across the center line in an effort to prevent Smith from passing, but we had too much speed and managed to pass with ease by pulling slightly onto the berm of the highway. When the white man got to a phone booth, he called the police and told them that Smith had run him off the highway.

Subsequently, we were pulled over about ten minutes later by two highway policeman. They didn't ask for Smith's driver's license. They just ordered him out of the car. Smith stepped out of the car with both hands in the air. I was ordered out of the car as well. But seeing I was just an eleven-year-old kid, I was told to beat it. Frightened, I cut across the field towards home, running as swiftly as I could before they changed their minds. I stopped suddenly when I heard a loud cry. They were not after me. They were too busy kicking and beating Smith on the street. I stood behind a tall, thick hedge and watched.

While Smith was down on the ground begging for mercy, I saw one of the policeman kick him repeatedly in the face. After they had beaten him almost to death, he was then taken to jail. Smith served thirty days on the county farm for not letting a white man pass him on the road.

I went home with a lifetime memory of what I saw. Afterwards, I hated every white policeman. I hated every white man. The story I read in the First Reader was a lie. A policeman was not my friend. White policemen, in particular, were not black people's friends. Every time I saw a white policeman in Greenwood on Saturday nights, he was beating a Negro for little or nothing. I couldn't conceive a man like that being my friend.

After witnessing the beating I walked the three miles from Greenwood to my home. I was frightened of every car that occasionally came down Highway U.S.E. I kept thinking the same thing might happen to my brothers, my father, or me. I have said from that day on, no white man would ever beat me to death, especially a white policeman. I would rather die fighting back. Many black men I knew felt the same way, because there was no justice for our people in Mississippi.

Smith's bossman could have made an issue of the maltreatment of him; instead he permitted Smith to serve the thirty days for nothing. When his time was up his boss went to pick him up. Smith died six months later from that beating, which resulted in a severe head injury. The colored people who knew Smith said he never fully recovered. It was said that he had no medical treatment the whole time he stayed on the county farm.

And rarely did Mississippi police officers leave a Negro physically capable of making statements. Negro men would be found dead, discarded like rubbish, and there would be no trial. It didn't help a Negro man to be taken to jail for his own "protection" against a lynch mob, because white officers/Klansmen would turn their backs, allowing the terror-stricken man to be dragged from his cell.

There was neither justice nor protection in the state of Mississippi for black people. The law was on the side of whites. And whites who challenged the system in defense of a Negro suffered through hell for it. That is one reason the system lasted as long as it did. Good-hearted white people who actually tried to help a Negro could lose their jobs, have mortgages foreclosed, or even be killed. And their peers would have subjected such "nigger lovers" to a righteous lecture about the ways of the land: "We're not going to change, no matter what the rest of the United States does, because niggers are not as good as white folks. Our children will never go to school with nigger children."

White kids rode the big yellow school buses, while Daddy, his precocious younger brother, David, and their sister, Viola, had to walk in the rain, the cold, and the sleet to the Essie Plantation School for Colored Children. Later they walked along Highway

23

49E to Broad Street High School in Greenwood, while the white kids rode comfortably past them to the all-white Greenwood High.

One day in 1944, I was by myself and walking backwards thumbing a ride, when a group of white students yelled out of the bus,"Walk, ol' darkie." I tried not to let their name calling bother me. But then another bus load of white kids passed, uttering even nastier names. I stopped trying to thumb a ride and began walking swiftly down the highway. I walked the entire three miles home that day. When I got home, I was tired, hungry, and angry. I entered the door with a hung-jaw expression, so noticeable that my mother immediately asked,"What's wrong, Son?"

The look on my face caused her to look at me with a frightened expression, plus I was talking to myself.

"It's just not fair. It's just not fair." I kept saying this over and over as I walked through the house.

"What is not fair, Son?" my mother asked as she followed me. I placed my books on the dresser drawer and turned to walk into the kitchen, before being halted by my mother.

"What is wrong with you, Boy?" she asked with a kind of concern that could easily be interpreted as weariness.

"Nothing is wrong with me, Mama," I said, pushing past her gently. She stood blocking me, insisting I give her an answer that made sense.

"Mama, I don't think it's fair that colored children have to walk to school in the rain and cold, while white children ride the buses that all our taxes helped to buy."

Mama's eyes filled with tears. I knew that she understood how difficult it was for us children, and had hoped we wouldn't think too much about the disadvantages, and just do the best we could under the caste system of Mississippi.

She dried her eyes with a cotton sack apron and said, "Come on and eat, Son. Someday things will be better."

The faith that my parents had in me was the symbol of everlasting hope. I sat down at the big home-made table covered with a cloth made from the cotton sacks we had used for picking cotton a few weeks earlier. For dinner Mama had a big pot of black-eyed peas. We also had corn bread and baked sweet potatoes.

"Eat all you want, Son."

No doubt my father ate heartily in spite of his anger, because it must have been some comfort to hear my grandmother say, "Eat all you want, Son." Normally, he would have had to restrict himself so there would be enough food for the rest of the family. Many nights he went to bed hungry. That day, though, Daddy might have eaten all he desired, but it wouldn't have been nearly enough soul food to diminish the emptiness he must have felt in the pit of his belly. For it wasn't food that he required most. Daddy's appetite was for a sense of optimism that his life would be better than what he was then experiencing in a land where boundless opportunity was given to white-skinned immigrants but systematically denied to their darker brothers.

On that day, as Daddy ate a meatless supper of black-eyed peas, corn bread, and sweet potatoes from a ten-cent, ivory Woolworth's plate and drank water from a Mason jar, he thought about the white kids on that school bus. He thought about how they could go to school at the end of the summer and not wait until after the cotton was gathered, in late October or November, as he and his brothers were required to do. He grew angrier and more impatient with the unfairness of the Mississippi educational system, which said, by its lack of interference, that it was okay

25

if Negro children did not attend school for the state-required number of days, because King Cotton came first. According to this system, it didn't matter that many black children in Mississippi could not adequately read or write.

Nevertheless, the little schooling Daddy was receiving made him thirst for more knowledge. The black teachers at his for-colored-children-only school truly inspired him. He was envious of the more fortunate Negro children who looked down on him and other sharecropper kids because they were poor and had to leave school to toil in the fields. These snobby colored children, who were the sons and daughters of house painters, truck drivers, ministers, principals, and schoolteachers, treated Daddy almost as badly as the white kids who rode past him each morning on the school buses. Daddy didn't like this group of Negro kids at all, and especially hated it when they called him "Big Lips" and "Country Boy." He got into plenty of fights with them.

One school year Daddy's fledgling self-esteem was given a major boost that turned his life around. He was attending Broad Street High School.

I entered the mathematics class and sat in the back row. The test papers were passed out immediately. My paper had a "90" written above "100," meaning I had gotten ninety problems out of a hundred correct.

My fellow classmates looked at me with surprise and said "Ahhhhh" all at the same time. The teacher then put my grade on the blackboard, making an example of it and comparing it to the other students' grades. Then we all went over the problems together.

"Andrew has been here only two days this week," the teacher said.

The students said, "Ahhhhh" again, but not all this time, just a few. The teacher then taught that day's lesson. I paid close attention. When the bell rang for the next class, I got ready to leave.

"Stay here, Andrew," my teacher requested. I remained in the room to wait for whatever he had to say.

"Come up to my desk, I want to talk to you." I walked towards him, mindful of the gray dust that covered the tops of my old shoes — my only pair.

Smiling, he asked, "How did you do it?" He questioned me as though he was puzzled, truly puzzled for the first time in his life. "I have already checked with your other teachers. You have not made under a 'B' in any of your classes. How did you do it?" he asked me again.

"I don't know, Sir, except that I'm determined to achieve my objectives. I don't want to pick cotton all of my life like my parents. And I have always wanted to become a teacher. I want to help other boys and girls like myself. I want to prove to myself, my parents, and all those who have deprived me, and those who helped me as well. I guess to put it simply, Sir, I just want to be somebody, whatever my ability will permit me to be." Then I self-consciously half-turned away, making ready for the next class change. He stopped me with a hand on my arm.

"I am proud of you, Andrew. I wish every Negro child in my class had your ambition. I'm sure you'll achieve your objectives." He then extended his hand.

I received his long slender fingers within my big callused hand. We shook hands firmly.

I thanked him and walked out of the room in time to reach my next class. I was the last to enter and drew the attention of everyone in the room. I momentarily felt embarrassed as all eyes watched me take a seat behind my desk.

The teacher said, "Good morning, Andrew." I replied in like manner.

Turning my head slightly to the right to get a direct focus on the blackboard, I was surprised. Written on the board were two of the highest marks made in English. An "85" and an "80." The "85" was my grade and the "80" was Annie Green's. I was happy about my achievement. It went that way all that day. I had made the honor roll and it wasn't too long before it had circulated around the entire school, because at the end of the day there were smiles where there used to be slurs and disassociative attitudes.

Having being born poor and black in the Deep South, I was well aware of my limitations. I knew too well what was expected of me, which was nothing.

But I wanted to become so much more.

On many plantations it was customary to ring a bell to awaken the tenants in the morning. This was usually around four o'clock.

Mama's Plantation

Although my parents both grew up in Mississippi, their lives were very different. Arella Love, my mother, was born March 29, 1935, on the Wildwood Plantation. She grew up not far from there on Jimmy Cole's plantation in Money, Mississippi. Her childhood experiences were unlike Daddy's; while he was dirt poor, Mama was allowed certain advantages by the owners of the plantation where she lived.

Because of their contrasting experiences in Mississippi, their union was a successful one. Although Daddy was determined to succeed, it was Mama who, during the difficult times, always saw the rainbow. My father's achievements were influenced greatly by Mama's unfailing optimism, an attitude she had gotten from her parents and from her experiences as a colored girl on the Cole plantation. Through the many stories she told over the years, I was able to understand what Mama's life was like in comparison to Daddy's.

Mama's parents are Velma and Hamp Love. My grandmother is a dark-skinned woman with short, coarse hair and a flat nose. Even as a young woman she stood no taller than four feet, eight inches tall. Many people on the Cole plantation fondly referred to her as "Little Bit." On the other hand, Granddaddy is tall and fair-skinned, with keen features and hair that tends to be more straight than curly. Granddaddy was often referred to as "Bit" or "Big Bit." They have always made an interesting-looking couple.

In his prime, Granddaddy was a small-time bootlegger who, by moonlight, sold whiskey in quart-sized Mason jars. To appear legitimate, he periodically sharecropped and drove a tractor in Mr. Cole's cotton fields. Grandmama picked cotton until the late 1950s, when they opened a little grocery store at the front of their three-room house, which was surrounded by acres of cotton.

Although each had only a third- or fourth-grade education, they did very well and amassed a little nest egg through their entrepreneurial abilities; they also raised hogs, chickens, cows, and vegetables. This meant that they lived better than the average colored sharecroppers in Mississippi. In addition to having an automobile when most plantation coloreds were walking to town, Granddaddy also had a pick-up truck in which to haul his goods around.

Mama's only sibling was a hardheaded, meddlesome younger brother, William. As brothers and sisters do, they fought, argued, and played together. Both took after their father in appearance, having his high Indian cheekbones, wide mouth, and fair complexion.

In 1941, when my mother was six years old, her family moved to Mr. Jimmy Cole's plantation. The Cole plantation was made up of two sections, Nebo and Moles Lake. Nebo was heavily treed and not so suitable for growing cotton, whereas Moles Lake was chiefly flat and more easily planted. Moles Lake is where most of Mama's growing up took place.

Mr. Cole was well liked by the Negroes on his place. But, like nearly all the white plantation owners in Mississippi, he wasn't entirely fair at settlement time. He had one set of books, and it was regularly in his favor. Mr. Cole's bookkeeping tactics may very well have been unscrupulous; however, he wasn't known to exploit the coloreds who worked for him. Colored people on his place generally were grateful for their pay, because they didn't have to slave like dogs just to receive next-to-nothing wages. Mr. Cole was fairer than was customary for a white plantation owner in Mississippi, and he was respected for it.

If a worker stood up to Mr. Cole, he would fare a lot better than if he kept his mouth shut; my grandfather would argue with his boss because he also kept his own books. After some arguing, Mr. Cole would grudgingly settle up right. It wasn't easy arguing with Mr. Cole. First, he was a businessman; second, he was white; and third, this was Mississippi. Negroes didn't argue with white folks in Mississippi. But somehow my grandfather got around all three major hurdles, and to his own satisfaction. Of course, Granddaddy receiving his due was primarily because Mr. Cole was a decent man who, for the most part, liked the Negroes who worked for him. He liked and respected my grandfather a great deal.

When Old Man Cole moved to California, he allowed his son-in-law, Mr. Jeff, to acquire a portion of his land, the Moles Lake section. But before he left, Mr. Cole asked my grandfather and his family to move with him. Granddaddy politely refused, saying that Mississippi was his home.

Mr. Jeff had married Miss Riley, one of Mr. Cole's daughters. Surprisingly, Mr. Jeff was as well liked by the coloreds on the plantation as Mr. Cole had been. Not surprisingly, his practice at settlement time was the same. Consequently, my grandfather also had money disputes with Mr. Jeff.

On those occasions, after an argument with Granddaddy, Mr. Jeff would curl his lips in exasperation and say, "Hamp, you just think you're a white man."

Defiantly, my grandfather would earnestly say, "No, Mr. Jeff, I'm just a man."

Mama heard my grandfather reply this way one glorious summer day as she sat reading and swaying on a porch swing at the back of the house. She was covered by the shadows of a screened enclosure and could listen without being seen. Granddaddy and Mr. Jeff were having some kind of quarrel about money. Mama peered over the back of the swing. She was astonished by how her father stood firm. His mouth was set in an angry but determined line. Mr. Jeff, a slight man with brown hair, stood on the other side of a barbed-wire fence looking red-faced and mad. The two men were locked eyeball to eyeball; neither was willing to yield to the other. Mama said Granddaddy didn't seem the least bit frightened of a white man who could summon a lynch mob with the shrill of a whistle if he were so inclined.

While Mama watched from her protected spot on the rotting porch, Granddaddy reached into his pocket and then showed Mr. Jeff some figures written on a quarter sheet of folded notebook paper. Mr. Jeff looked over the neatly written figures. His face appeared to smooth as he calculated. Soon he was reaching in his pocket to compensate my grandfather equitably. Mama said Granddaddy took the money, counted it, and put it in his pocket. There was not another word spoken aloud as both men turned away, muttering under their breaths.

Probably each man called the other a son of a bitch. Mr. Jeff got into his truck and sped off, leaving a cloud of dust. Granddaddy went back to tending the hogs at the back of the house. Mama returned to her swinging and reading, never once fearing that her father would be lynched in the middle of the night. If this had happened on the plantation where Daddy grew up, the outcome would have been much different.

On the Cole plantation there was nothing for Mama to fear. Granddaddy and Mr. Jeff had reached an understanding years ago. From time to time, Granddaddy simply had to remind Mr. Jeff that he was dealing with a man and not a boy. If the other coloreds on the Cole plantation didn't know any better than to stand up for themselves, that was their own problem.

The primary reason that the Negroes respected these white owners is that they didn't allow the sheriff or any other whites to come onto the plantation and intimidate their workers. Back when this was a common practice, Mr. Cole and Mr. Jeff occupied places of distinction in the minds of Negroes in Leflore County. Not having to worry about being lynched or harassed made the Cole plantation a haven for the Negroes who lived there.

Something else unusual about this plantation was that Mr. Jeff and Mr. Cole would take it upon themselves to go back and apologize to coloreds who worked for them, if they felt they had treated someone unfairly or talked to someone too harshly. My grandfather was apologized to yearly, and usually around settlement time, which was when he and the owners locked horns.

Mr. Jeff would come back after about a half hour and say, "Hamp, I didn't mean it when I told you to get the hell off my land. I was just mad." (That is how Mama described those occasions.) Following a heated exchange, when Granddaddy would have replied, "Mr. Jeff, I'll be glad to get off your land and out of that ol' 'piecey' falling-down house of yorns," the apologies would come. After the arguments they always made up, these two men in Mississippi, one Negro and the other white.

By 1947, my mother, Arella, was a bookworm who would read anything she could curl her long, slender fingers around. Through reading she would visit far-off mystical places or be captivated by wild adventures. She especially loved comic books. She read them by the stack, and she always had a supply of the latest editions. Superman was her favorite comic hero.

On Saturdays when Arella and William received their two-dollar allowance, they would jump eagerly into the back seat of the car for the weekly ride to Greenwood. Once there, my grandparents would give them the same instructions: "Don't get into any trouble." Then they all agreed on the time and place to meet later that day. They parted ways on Johnson Street, the heart of Greenwood's black community.

Jews owned the buildings on Johnson Street, but Negro entrepreneurs rented many of them. And some of everything could be bought, from the latest styles at Stanley's department store to hot fish sandwiches at the Fish Market. Negro couples who wanted to dance or have a sit-down dinner were accommodated at the Sunshine Cafe. Johnson Street was a busy and bustling place every Saturday, all year round.

Colored folks, usually dressed in their Sunday best, were all over the sidewalk and spilling into the street. It was a grand and carefree time, when everyone could just have fun and not think about the burden of being black in Mississippi. It was also when people got updates and a chance to compare stories about what was happening to Negroes in other towns and on other plantations. They would come in from places such as Tchula, Grenada, Slaughter, Minter, and Greenville. Country folks and city folks stood and conversed, creating little vignettes.

Mingled with teachers and other professionals were sharecroppers, cotton pickers and laborers from all the nearby plantations. "I'm from so and so. Where are y'all from?" This could be heard over and over, as smiling people made their way around clusters of others. Colored people of various shades, going up and down parallel uneven sidewalks, laughed and greeted people they hadn't seen in a while or since the previous Saturday. Every Saturday on Johnson Street, colored folks were happy to see one another.

Arella and William would make their way through all the gladhanding. With two dollars deep in their dungaree pockets, they would scurry along, weaving under and around groups of colored greeters. Sometimes they would stop and talk to colored children they knew who had also come in from the country. But if these kids wouldn't do what the brother and sister wanted, they would have to be abandoned. Arella and William had been told to stay together.

With her allowance for doing chores, Arella would buy herself a Baby Ruth, a Hershey bar, an Almond Joy, an orange Nehi pop, an RC Cola, a "delicious and refreshing" Coca-Cola, and, for five cents, a huge strawberry ice cream cone. Carrying a brown paper bag loaded with her goodies, which would be rationed for the entire week (if William didn't find her hiding place), she would eat her cone. Slowly she savored each lick, for as long as the summer heat permitted. By midday, she and William would take in a movie at the Walthall Theater. Her brother would have eaten up all his stuff by the day's end. The only thing he would take home would be a bellyache.

The Walthall Theater catered to both white and colored, but on alternate days. Across town the Leflore Theater and the Paramount Theater were strictly for whites only. Of course, they were much nicer than the Walthall. At any rate, Saturday was colored-only day at the Walthall, and Arella and William could catch a cowboy picture there.

When the Love family traveled back up Highway 49E, to connect with the dirt road lit only by their car's headlights, they would have had a full day. Two streaming beams of light would startle all nighttime creatures caught unaware as the family returned to their shack, furnished from the Greenwood furniture store and owned by Mr. Cole.

Arella and William did pick cotton, but their earnings were not a requirement for the family resources. When Mama and her brother wanted to buy something extra special in town, that is how they would earn the money. So, unlike Daddy, who had to miss school because of the cotton fields, Mama and Uncle William attended school for the same number of months the white kids did.

And, at a time when white Mississippi plantation owners routinely designated a large shack or a Negro church as the school for colored children, Mr. Cole built an exceptionally nice facility for the children on his plantation. The Nebo Plantation School for Colored Children was a seven-room, red-painted wooden building nestled in a thicket of woods that was interrupted by acres of cotton patches. Alongside the school building, which included an auditorium and a stage for plays and school programs, was a nice red house for the principal and his family. Arella and

William attended the Nebo Plantation School until the eighth grade, after which they were required to attend Money Vocational High School for Colored Children.

Mr. Cole hired a Negro named Mr. Celeste to be the principal of the school. Everyone respectfully referred to him as Professor Celeste. The professor, a rather tall man of fair complexion, brought along as his assistant his wife, an attractive cinnamon-skinned woman who wore her long hair in a bun secured by bobby pins at the nape of her neck. An older gray-haired woman named Mrs. Burton taught at the school as well.

Arella especially liked Mrs. Burton for coming to her defense when she got a belt whipping by the professor. She and her best friend, Essie, had gotten into a childish scramble out on the playground. An argument over a swing resulted in a pushing and shoving match. Unfortunately, Essie lost when Arella, who could fight as well as any of the boys, delivered a one-two punch. The professor, without asking who started it, called Arella into his office and gave her a few lashes. After the whipping, he sent her back outside to the playground. A proud child, Arella sniffled indignantly as the other kids observed the welts rising on her bare, skinny legs.

Mrs. Burton, having seen Essie instigating the fight, let the young professor know he was wrong. Later that day, my grandfather, after viewing my mother's bruises, gave the professor "a good talking to." My mother never liked the professor one bit after that. She did, however, feel a lot better after she had been vindicated, because at that time adults rarely spoke up for kids, even if they felt a child had been unjustly treated. Adults, especially teachers and parents, were always right. The premise was that if you got an undeserved whipping, sooner or later you would deserve one anyway.

Other teachers occasionally substituting at the school were Professor Celeste's nephew; Mrs. Burton's son, Leonard; and her daughter, Miss Burton. Miss Burton, a tall, nearly white-looking young woman, had a naughty habit of stealing the goodies out of Arella and William's well-stocked lunches of ham sandwiches, potato chips, and oatmeal cookies or bologna and cheese and crackers. She never raided the other kids' meager lunches. One morning Arella caught the young slip of a teacher red-handed, helping herself to cookies. Without forethought, she angrily snatched her lunch from the startled and embarrassed Miss Burton. After that, Arella and William didn't have any more problems with the sticky-fingered teacher.

It is amazing how different my parents' lives were, considering that they both lived in Leflore County. My father never played with white children, and when he came into contact with them, it was not a positive experience. Being called "blackie," "nigger," and "coon" by white kids passing on a school bus further reinforced the negative image of a racist Mississippi and made him feel inferior.

My mother and Uncle William, however, were best friends with two white kids, Mary and Floydeen, who also happened to be brother and sister. Those friendships ended sadly, one because of an accidental shooting and the other because of my grandmother's interference.

Mary and Floydeen had good parents, which is the primary reason the children's friendships flourished in the 1940s in spite of the racial climate in Mississippi. Of course, by law the children were not permitted to attend the same schools, but they played together after school for years.

Arella and Mary played house with their Christmas dolls, and had tea parties with their pink-and-white floral dish sets bought at Woolworth's. They went bareback riding on brown and black mares on the dirt roads that divided the cotton fields. They told each other secrets and laughed at each other's jokes. Their love was like that of sisters and was blind to color.

Ironically, it wasn't Mary's mother who apprised the daughter approaching her teen years that her friendship with the little colored girl would have to cease because of Mississippi's social order. It was because of my grandmother that the relationship ended.

"A-rella," my grandmother instructed my mother the spring she turned thirteen, "now that you and Mary are getting older, it's time you start calling her 'Miss Mary.'" My mother, having enjoyed a unique friendship with the white girl, couldn't give credence to what she was hearing. Naturally, she was aware that colored people were treated differently from whites, but she and Mary had been friends a long time and had never gotten into all that. When she and her brother visited at their white friends' house, they were treated well.

"Mama, we're friends," Arella said in defense against the order given. "I don't have to call Mary 'Miss' anything. We get along just fine."

"Yes, you do, too, gal, and that is what I want you to call her from now on," commanded my grandmother on that fateful day.

That was the end of the conversation and the end of a precious friendship. My mother, rather than have to address her best friend as "Miss Mary," chose to dissolve the bond they had shared. She did it by ignoring the puzzled white girl whenever she came over to visit, until Mary stopped coming altogether. Arella never discussed the matter with her friend, and Mary never learned why Arella was suddenly so cold toward her. Both girls were deeply hurt.

At the time, my mother didn't see the point in discussing the situation with Mary, because she felt there was nothing either of them could do about it. Grandmama had told her what the rules were in Mississippi, and she simply couldn't abide by them. She and Mary had not only been best friends but, Arella felt, equals. It would have been insulting to explain that "since I'm a nigger and less than you, I now have to call you 'Miss Mary.'" Arella could not bring herself to make such a humiliating remark, even to her dearest friend, who just happened to be white.

Years later, after they had both grown up, the last thing my mother heard about her friend was that she had married an insurance salesman and moved to Jackson. Mama has always wished that my grandmother had not interfered. Of course, sooner or later the issue would have surfaced, and the friendship might have been altered anyway. We will never know.

The tragedy that ended William and Floydeen's friendship was a hunting accident. Up until then, like all country boys they had shot marbles, played cowboys and Indians, ridden tires, climbed trees, fished, and gone rabbit and pheasant hunting. They were practically inseparable.

Early one Saturday morning the boys got up and ate a big breakfast of biscuits, sausages, and eggs my grandmother had prepared for them. Their plans were to go bird hunting. Floydeen had spent the night with William, and they had giggled and talked long into the night before falling asleep in William's cotton-stuffed bed at the back of the house.

That morning, eager to get into the woods, they were raising a ruckus with their laughter and jostling around. The boys were developing into men, no longer needing fathers as chaperones to keep them from horsing around and scaring the game away. They left grinning, slamming the door to the back porch.

42

Just as the boys were about to cut to the path through the cotton field, Grandmama remembered she had some chore she wanted William to do first. "A-rella, go call William back," she said to Mama.

From the kitchen window, Arella could see William and Floydeen making their way one at a time along the path. She was washing dishes, and she knew that whatever it was Grandmama wanted William to do, she would be stuck doing it if she didn't get him back. She dropped the dishrag and ran through the house. Pushing the screen door open, she went out the back door onto the enclosed porch. Through another screen door she leaped over two wooden steps onto the grass. Then she stopped.

To this day my mother can't explain what happened to her. She could see the boys, who were within earshot, but she couldn't speak. Only gasps of air came from her silent lips when she tried to yell her brother's name.

"William, William, William" came out in a croak when she tried with all her might to override her muted vocal cords. That fateful day, the boys did not hear her and kept on walking. Arella watched them with wide eyes as they entered the woods. She went back into the house feeling a strange foreboding. Nothing like this had ever happened to her before.

"You call William?" Grandmama questioned her as she swept the kitchen floor.

"Yes, Mama, I did," Arella answered breathlessly before turning back to the white porcelain dishpan that held the morning dishes. There was no inside plumbing; a gas stove heated water for bathing and dishwashing. A hand-primed water pump sat at the edge of the road that skirted the house.

Arella poured more hot water into the soap-filled pan. For some unknown reason she felt worried. "He didn't hear me, Mama," she explained to her mother. Then she picked up the dishrag and began to wash the breakfast plates. Periodically, she peeked out the window at the woods.

After a couple of hours had passed and Arella had finished her housework, she decided to read a comic book on the porch swing. She was hoping the reading would take her mind off William and Floydeen. She was also beginning to believe that her uneasiness had been unfounded. Her brother and Floydeen had gone hunting many times before and nothing bad had happened to them, although dozens of rabbits and birds had seen their last season.

As soon as she walked out onto the porch she heard the wailing. It was an awful sound, and it was coming from just beyond the cotton field. Flinging the screen door open, she screamed for Grandmama to come quickly.

"Mama, something is wrong," she yelled over her shoulder as the homemade door crashed against the inside of the house. Bursting through the other screen door, she again leaped off the porch. This time she was yelling her brother's name at the top of her lungs. Too late, her voice was back and betraying her heartsick soul. My grandmother jumped up from a cane-backed chair, which fell with a thud onto the unpainted wooden floor. Grandmama, who had been about to nod off, had been sitting in the back bedroom listening to the radio and snapping beans for canning. Alerted by her daughter's desperate cry, she was out both doors before they swung closed. Spilled green beans and a silver pail were left rolling around the upended chair.

Uncle William was covered with blood when they reached him in the middle of the cotton field. No sound came from his wide-open mouth. But something dreadful had happened. His

44

terror-stricken eyes told them that, as he looked soundlessly from his mother to his sister. Something horrible had happened to Floydeen.

William could only gasp for air as the sweat and blood dripped around his mouth. He looked back and forth from his sister to his mother as he tried to tell them.

"Boy, what's wrong with you?" asked my grandmother as she helped her son stand up. "And where is Floydeen?" William was sinking to the ground, about to pass out. Arella quickly got on the other side of her brother. She took hold of the arm of his old brown coat, getting cold, sticky blood on her hands. She knew instantly that it had to be Floydeen's blood. Turning sideways, they made their way through the stripped cotton plants to the house.

Grandmama told my mother to run up to the store at the highway and fetch my grandfather. She ran like a gazelle. Arella didn't know what to tell her father when she spotted him sitting in a rocker talking with the other colored men on the wide sweeping porch. She figured they probably were discussing settlement time, because the cotton was all picked.

"What's the matter, A-rella," Granddaddy asked slowly in his southern drawl. He stood and threw the broomstick straw he was chewing to the floor. He had become alarmed at the sight of his daughter running up to him, and his face registered it. He knew that if Velma had sent one of the kids looking for him something was wrong.

While the other colored men looked on, Mama told Grand-daddy that Uncle William and Floydeen had gone hunting and something had happened. She told him that her brother was all right but that he was covered with blood. From the look in his eyes she knew he understood. She was telling him that William was covered with Floydeen's blood.

When they got back to the house, Grandmama had William in a tub full of hot water. He was now crying hysterically. Grandmama told Granddaddy that William told her he and Floydeen had rigged their shotguns to go off in case they saw a bird. But somehow, as they were walking through the brush, William had tripped. His gun went off, hitting Floydeen in the head.

Instantly, Granddaddy was out the door. He went up to Floydeen's house to get Mr. Floyd. When they got back, they parked the truck and went out into the woods. Two fathers, one colored, one white, crossed the cotton field in search of a son. Granddaddy said they found Floydeen's body lying beside a tree. The back of his head had been blown off. Blood was splattered everywhere, on the grass, the leaves, the bushes, and the surrounding trees, and Floydeen's brains were dripping from the branch of a cypress tree. It was a horrendous sight. Mr. Floyd had dropped to his knees and sobbed, then cradled the lifeless body of his dead son — his youngest child, William's best friend.

The police were never called; only Mr. Cole was informed of the incident. He and Mr. Floyd came to the house to question my uncle. William cried and hiccupped as he recounted the story. He was grieving heavily, and was probably afraid a white lynch mob would hang him in the very tree sprayed by Floydeen's brains. My mother and my grandparents also were worried. Floydeen's family was grief-stricken — and, accident or not, the colored family didn't know how the white family would react. Other coloreds on the plantation were worried as well. They told my grandfather that he should "take that boy away. Take him to Chicago."

"They're going to kill him, Bit," one of his friends said. Grand-daddy, never being a man to run, said no, he wouldn't send his son away. It had been an accident.

My grandparents attended Floydeen's funeral. Mr. Cole was there as well. Floydeen's older brother, Travis, was there, and his sister, Mary, was beside him. Uncle William remained at home, too distraught to say farewell to his friend. Mama stayed with her brother, who, now too quiet, had been in bed for nearly a week. Off and on, he had slept restlessly between nightmares.

In a gesture atypical of the era, after the funeral Floydeen's parents walked over to my grandparents and embraced them. Everyone wept openly. They told my grandparents not to worry, saying that they believed William's story. They also said they knew how much Floydeen and William had loved each other. And that was that.

If such a situation had occurred on my father's plantation, I would never have been born, because Daddy would have been lynched. Tragic as it is, this story underscores the vast differences between the lives of my parents and the events that shaped them. My mother's perception of whites in Mississippi was formed by her experiences, and the sharing of these stories with my father provided him with a different perspective on the question of racism in the state.

For a colored girl in Mississippi, my mother lived a very good life. And this wasn't just because my grandparents were hard-working and committed parents, but also because they lived on the Cole plantation, where the white owners were exceptional in their treatment of the Negroes on their place.

Mama and Uncle William grew up and eventually got over the loss of their childhood friends. They had other friends, colored friends, although none as close to them as Mary and Floydeen had been. Uncle William spent a couple of years in the army. He later moved to Chicago, married twice, and broke a lot of hearts. When he was in his late forties he moved back to Mississippi, and now lives in Jackson. Every now and then he talks about Floydeen.

My mother was married briefly to a man named Willie King. She was about eighteen years old when she fell in love for the first time. She really wanted to go to college, but my grandmother, not seeing the point, wouldn't permit it. After all, her daughter and son had obtained three times more schooling than she and my grandfather had. She saw this as quite an achievement. My mother was disappointed, because she was a very good student, excelling in math. She could have become anything she wanted.

But in 1954 Mama instead married Willie King, a tractor driver, with whom she had a baby girl, my oldest sister, Bernice. Mama told us later that she had not known that the man she married could barely read or write his name. After they moved to Indianapolis, she found out he was illiterate. Also, he couldn't keep a job, so their refrigerator stayed bare.

Mama wasn't used to being hungry and, besides, she was pregnant. She wrote to her parents, saying she wanted to come back to Mississippi. They went to Western Union and wired her some money. Mama came back, had the baby, and got a divorce. The marriage had lasted six months.

The Army taught me a lot...the experience of living with all kinds of people broadened my knowledge of people in general.

A Colored

A Colored Soldier

Daddy was in the eleventh grade at Broad Street High School when he received his induction papers. The year was 1952, and he was twenty-one years old. Although his grades were above average, he had not completed high school. It isn't clear whether my father entered school late or lost several years of schooling along the way. What is indisputable is that for several generations the Mississippi cotton fields deferred or ended educational opportunities for children of Negro sharecroppers like my father. However, Daddy was as eager to become a soldier as he was determined to become a schoolteacher. Both objectives were part of his mission to stay out of the cotton fields.

Daddy's oldest brother, Clevester, had served in World War II. Now, during the Korean War, it was Daddy's turn to serve in the Colored Unit of the United States Army. He remembered how excited he had been when his brother had finally come home, how Clevester had been so well fed that he looked "fat and healthy"; he was not "half hungry-looking" like the Negroes on the plantation. To my father this meant that there would be plenty to eat in the army. Now he would not have to drink a lot of water to inflate his belly because there wasn't sufficient food.

51

In the days before Daddy was to report to Jackson, he spent time pulling sweet potatoes from the several rows they had planted for winter eating. He ran his big callused hands over each potato, knocking off the dirt before throwing it into the wicker basket that was placed with each step between himself and his father as they made their way down the rows. They were determined to gather all the vegetables before Daddy's departure.

Now that his two hearty sons weren't going to be able to help out, Granddaddy Jordan had decided to stop sharecropping and move into town. In fact, many of their neighbors, the McCoys, the Millers, the McDonalds, and others, had left the plantation a few years earlier. Several had even bypassed Greenwood and moved on to places like Chicago, Los Angeles, Cleveland, and Detroit, where they would find better employment.

The migration of blacks from Mississippi plantations was also precipitated by the declining value of cotton as a crop. Now that synthetics and cheaper cotton could be purchased from overseas, black labor was no longer an economic necessity for southern states. As a result of the depression and the bottoming out of the cotton market, black labor was becoming less of a commodity in Mississippi.

Another major factor in the decreased need for black labor was the mechanization of cotton production. Shortly after World War I, laborers had begun to be replaced by machinery that could do the work faster and cheaper. First came the tractor, and then flame cultivators, machines that could clear a field for approximately thirty-five cents compared to the dollar a day paid to Negroes hoeing and singing "Sweet Chariot." By the 1940s, cotton harvesters were in use; one of these could outpick fifty Negroes.

So, the Negro families who had half starved all those years in near slave-like conditions were now out of work. Daddy was lucky to be army bound, considering that many Negro families who stayed in Greenwood later went on welfare. There was very little work available, the situation having been drastically reversed. Whereas before, whites would use intimidation and lynching to keep "their niggers" in the cotton fields, by the late 1950s and early 1960s they couldn't have cared less if every "nigger" left the state. My father needn't have worried about being relegated to the cotton fields, because Mississippi was no longer the Land of King Cotton.

Daddy labored hard that fall with his family in order to harvest the garden. As he yanked sweet potatoes from the earth, he let his mind wander over the stories Clevester had shared with them about a Negro's life in the military — a life that was soon to be his own. He also remembered how much his brother had changed.

I walked into the house and saw a pair of GI boots. Right away I knew they were Clevester's. I ran into our bedroom. He wasn't there. I heard someone coming from the hen house. It was Mama. She was singing her favorite song, "I'm Sending Up My Timber." I think it was a song that she had made up. She sounded happy. Her oldest son was home.

"Where is he, Mama?" I asked impatiently.

"He's gone to the sto'," she explained. "You'll see him tonight."

I couldn't wait. I jumped on the old bike and rode, as fast as I could, the mile to the store. I was fourteen years old when my brother Clevester returned from the war, and I was proud of him.

When I had gotten within a hundred yards, I saw him with some other people. He looked well, for he was fat — and so was every Negro soldier who came home. My brother was just as I had pictured him to be.

He was talking to Jack Pot, whose real name was Tom Anderson, but everyone called him Jack Pot. I never knew why exactly, except perhaps it was because he was extremely dark-skinned. Anyway, I rode up on my bike and stopped beside by brother and said, "Hi." He said something. I gather he had spoken to me before he resumed talking to Mr. Jack Pot. Mr. Pot spoke too, then he turned to my brother and asked, "Clevester, don't you know who that boy is?"

"No," my brother replied as he looked at me again. "No, I don't, Jack."

"You really don't?" Jack Pot looked at him now with a concerned expression.

"No, I don't," my brother repeated.

Then, "Who is he?" Clevester asked this as he looked at me closely.

"That's your brother, Cleve. That's Andrew."

My brother placed his right index finger in the corner of one eye, and left index finger in the corner of the other eye, in an attempt to clear his vision.

"Boy, you sure have grown. Damn it, how old are you?" He asked this as his blood-shot eyes moved up and down me like radar searching for some means of identity, as he tried to adjust his eyes to my seemingly rapid growth at the same time.

"Do you have any money?" he asked as his red liquor eyes danced in his head.

"No," I replied quickly.

"Here." He gave me a fifty-cent piece.

"Okay, you better get on back home now. Tell Mama and Papa I'll be early tonight," he added.

I told him, "Okay." I jumped on the bike which now was shared by only four of us. I had kept it long enough.

When I reached my house, Papa had arrived and so had my other brothers, Will and David, as well as my sister, Viola. They were all excited about seeing Cleve. He was named after Papa. I told them, my parents, that he had promised to come home early that night. At about ten o'clock he did come. We kept him up most of the night asking questions about the war. He told us many things about the Army and his experiences.

He told us about the motion pictures that came from America to England and from other areas overseas. He said that, in them, black men were always the laughingstock. They were picture shows with black men wearing straw hats and overalls, and trousers with one leg shorter or longer than the other. In the middle of the conversation Papa asked, "What will you do now that you're out of the service, Son?"

"Well, Papa," Cleve said, pausing slightly for words. "I'm leaving for Cleveland, Ohio, next week. I can't stay around here anymore. I've seen too much." Then he went on while pacing the floor with both hands behind him. "A black man will never get justice in the South. To stay out of trouble, Papa, I'm leaving."

Papa nodded his head understandingly, then gave his oldest son his blessings. Cleve then went to bed and so did all of us. A week later my brother was gone, and my parents were happy that he was gone. They knew he wouldn't take much from whites and they feared for his life.

Black Mississippians didn't readily comprehend who the actual enemies were when their men fought under the flag of the United States of America. And it wasn't clear who white plantation owners considered to be their real enemies either, because German prisoners sent to plantations in the South were treated much better than Negro sharecroppers were. These "prisoners" had better accommodations than the Negroes, who lived in shacks that were sweltering in the summer and freezing in the winter.

German prisoners were granted adequate amounts of food to eat, while children of sharecroppers were routinely hungry, and they were afforded considerably better employment than the Negroes, who were granted work no one else was prone to do. While white German soldiers were being detained in the South, black-skinned citizens, the backbone of the Mississippi economy, were keeping the cotton sacks full, and begrudging the prisoners.

My father, nevertheless, was intensely pleased about being inducted into the army. He looked upon it with much anticipation and was earnest about having an opportunity to serve. Most important, though, it was presumably an opportunity to have a better life.

On November 22, I went to Jackson, Mississippi, for a physical examination. I was accepted and called to active duty on December 10, 1952. The Korean War was on, although much of it was over. However, there was still much to be done. I was the second in my family to enter the Army to fight the white man's war. My older brother had fought bravely in World War II. He had given his time in the Army, helping to win a victory that only enslaved him back home.

He and thousands of other black soldiers fought in France, Germany and other foreign places. They were promised justice, civil rights, and full citizenship once they got back to the states. They fought well in Poland, Japan, and England just as other Negroes had done in the Revolutionary War, the War of 1812, the Civil War, the Spanish American War, and in World War I. Negroes fought with pride and dignity for themselves and for their country. Their hope was that the United States would live up to its true meaning of the anthem,"land of the free and home of the brave." They hoped that by showing patriotism the United States would do the right thing toward the equality of black people, once Negroes had shown they were willing to fight and die for their country.

I don't believe black solders were particularly devastated about being treated as second-class citizens in the Army, so long as they had hope for a better tomorrow. But, like their ancestors in slavery time who were promised a mule and forty acres of land after the Civil War in payment for years of inhuman suffering, blacks coming home from wars since have seen little in reparations.

Mississippi black soldiers, in particular, came home only to find themselves still slaves. There were no decent jobs. They had become refugees in their own country and were forced by the economy to return to work akin to slavery. But no one black in Mississippi expected to be paid fair wages. Black soldiers, however, were surprised at not getting a better share, and many were not shared much of anything. They did indeed struggle to survive while the white man got richer.

Upon returning home, Negro soldiers of World War II found themselves subjected to the same type of treatment they had left to enter the military. The white man had used them again. They still could not vote as free men and women. They found themselves faced with all kinds of laws, unjust laws, such as poll taxes that pertained only to Negroes. And they had to take tests that were impossible to pass, because they had to interpret parts of the Mississippi Constitution the way the white man wanted it interpreted, and many times he couldn't interpret it himself.

He was still lynched by the Ku Klux Klan whenever he stepped out of line. No one from the state level to the Supreme Court did much about it or anything at all. He was not able to get jobs of his own choosing, in spite of his educational background. He could not stay in white-only hotels when traveling across the country for which he had fought so valiantly, whenever called to duty. The Germans, the Japanese and all other people were free in the United States. They even became the bosses of black people all over the country. They were the first hired over blacks in many factories throughout the United States, while black people became more and more subjected to handouts.

"No one will stop me from fulfilling my dreams," I said to myself as I rode the Greyhound bus to the Induction Center. I still wanted to become a soldier. Not knowing why really, except that I thought it was better than half eating and working on a plantation where only the white man benefited.

We arrived at the Induction Center about noon that day. We were taken immediately to lunch. Whites and blacks went to separate eating places. The blacks were sent to a Negro hotel in the slum area of the city. Meanwhile white soldiers went to one of the best hotels in the city, the Robert E. Lee Hotel in the center of Jackson, Mississippi — a hotel named after the Confederate general. After lunch, we were bussed back to the center for tests. At four o'clock, we went back to our respective hotels for dinner and for the night. We were not restricted, so I took the liberty to roam the city with some other fellows. We took in a movie. I don't remember what played that night. After the movie we walked back to the hotel where we were lodging for the night.

As I lay awake most of the night, I kept thinking about my parents, my girlfriend, but mostly my parents — my father, to be exact. I wondered if he would still try to farm without me to help him. I had already told him to keep my part of the money, if there was any to keep. I was also thinking about the old familiar tradition, segregation. I wondered why we were segregated and yet we were to be trained to fight together. Was it because they were free men and they wanted to flaunt the precious gift that I never knew I had for certain?

It must be great to be free, I thought to myself. I was beginning to believe it was an overstated word that had no apparent meaning. I felt I had never been truly free. How could it have meaning to me? Sure, I was free to go to black schools, black churches, black movies, and black cafes and hotels, the few we had. But this wasn't constitutional, not according to what I read in government, history and law books.

How can one man be free to go where he wishes while another one, because he is black, has limitations of movement that are twin to a strait jacket? I knew the system, perhaps better than any of the guys with me, and it just didn't make sense to me, except that the Constitution didn't apply to black people. However, it didn't say "white people only," it said "all the people," and I took that to mean black people, too, in spite of the injustices I had seen around me from childhood to manhood. But, somehow I wanted to have faith in my country and in the constitution, for if I lost faith entirely I wouldn't be a good soldier.

The next morning, we had chow early in order to get started all over again through the necessary routines. We had lunch in Jackson, then we were stuffed on the back of a truck and driven to the airport where we were to board a two engine Delta Airline plane to Fort Jackson, South Carolina, for basic training. There were two hundred fifty of us. We were soldiers now. It took us about three hours, no more than four, to reach Fort Jackson.

While in flight, the plane developed engine trouble. I was not afraid, perhaps because I had made up my mind that if it fell, I wouldn't know anything anyway. But in spite of my readiness, I reached into my shirt pocket and pulled out a Saint Christopher pin. Holding it in my left hand, facing me, with my right hand I made a cross on my chest. The pin had been given to me by one of the men I used to work for.

It was late that evening when we reached Fort Jackson. The big trucks were waiting for us. We were rushed on to the trucks and driven to the base. The first place we stopped was the mess hall. We ate chow and were taken to the company's supply room for bedding, then regrouped in sixes and told where we would sleep that night.

The night passed swiftly. We were called out at four o'clock the next morning for recruiting. The early rising didn't bother me as it seemed to have bothered the other guys. I was accustomed to it. I was used to getting up early to go to the cotton fields.

We were issued one pair of low shoes, ten uniforms, two pair of GI boots, and underwear among other things. I felt I had prospered when I received my supplies. I rushed to my living quarters and slipped anticipatively into my new shorts. They were the first I had ever owned by myself. My father and I would compete with other members of the family for shorts and socks. Of course, they belonged to my father. I would steal them if I saw them before he did. Anyway, having socks and those clothes was something new for me.

When we all had changed from civilian clothes into military uniforms the sergeant yelled, "Fall out, troopers." We fell out all right, like a bunch of old ladies. "Fall back in the barracks," the sergeant bellowed. "Now this time, fall out like you have backbone." He then screamed, "Fall out." We came out like a storm.

"Line up on me, troopers," he ordered, not smiling in the least. He paced himself about twenty spaces. He ordered us to form a formation of four lines, then marched us up and down the company's area for about fifteen minutes.

"All right, we are going to get haircuts. Then we are going to come back and shave that hair on your face. You are a soldier now, and you will look and act like one," he ordered.

"Attention!" We did our best to snap to attention. "Right face, forward march."

His voice was so deep that it seemed to vibrate through the ground. As we walked he counted, "One-two-three-four," and occasionally he would yell, "Get in step, Soldier." "You are not on Skid Row now. Walk with your chest out and your head up."

He was talking to me this time.

A Colored Soldier

I shuffled my steps to get in step with the man in front of me. He shuffled his steps to get in step with the man in front of him. This went on for about ten seconds because everyone was uncertain of his steps. The sergeant was still sounding his two-three rhythm. "Pick up your feet, soldier," he said, as he continued to count.

I had begun to get the swing of it when he shouted, "Halt, left face, at ease." Then, he said, "Fall out, and enter the building directly in front of you."

It was the barber shop, and there were five barbers there who didn't give a damn how they cut your hair. Fifty of us got a haircut in exactly thirty minutes. Each barber made no more than a few strokes on our heads. The barber started at my forehead and made a complete circle on the flat of my head, two strokes across, then around the sides — and a push off the chair. There were no lines or shape, just a plain, clean haircut called a GI cut. Every soldier received one, and he had no choice in the matter while he was wearing that uniform and in basic training.

Three weeks into the Army I saw a terrible thing happen to a black soldier. We were on the MI Rifle Range. A black soldier went AWOL from our company, C Company, 28th Infantry Division, Fort Jackson, South Carolina. The company had not had anyone go AWOL for a long time. A Negro soldier named Smith spoiled our good name. The policy was a beating of anyone who would do anything against the image of the company, by the entire company. While we were on the range, Smith came back to camp on his own. He was sent to the range immediately after his arrival under guard.

When he reached the range, he was placed under guard with a different man, another soldier. The soldier was white. His name was Bumgardner. I noticed right away the enjoyment he got out of it. He made Smith lie on the cold ground all afternoon. He didn't permit him to get any water. His orders were given to him by our company officer, whose name I don't remember. Each time Smith would rise to a semi-prone position, he was kicked in the side by the guard. I was terrified by this kind of action, so much so that I made it known to the other black soldiers in my company.

At four-thirty we all mounted the big trucks back to the company because it was too far to walk, but usually we did walk. There was talk on the truck among white soldiers about beating Smith when we got back to the company. The beating was to take place after dinner.

I said, "I think the man has suffered enough. Don't y'all agree?"

From my tone, anyone could see that I was not in favor of that kind of action.

Another black soldier said, "Yeah, Man, I think so, too."

We ate dinner in a hurry and made it back to our barracks. The white soldiers had already begun organizing themselves. They were ready.

One of them came up and said, "We want him."

"You want who?" I asked with full knowledge of who they wanted. Before he could answer I said, "No, you can't have him. I think the man has paid for his mistakes." Then I assured him by saying, "If you wish to fight him alone, you may, but there will be no crowd."

I then said, "The man will fight you. Won't you, Smith?"

I turned to Smith, and he agreed to fight each of them one at a time. But no one white soldier would fight him. It had to be the whole group.

At this point the white soldiers were ready to space themselves against us black soldiers. We welcomed the fight, but the company commander happened to be in the area and he became alarmed.

I spent three months in that company, and the beating of a black soldier or any soldier never came up again for going AWOL. I had seen too much of that kind of thing in Mississippi. I couldn't conceive this happening in the Army.

But it had happened before and had gone on for quite sometime according to some of the old soldiers' reports. I talked to one old Negro soldier about it.

"Why do you old soldiers permit this kind of thing to go on?" I asked.

He said, "When you have been in the Army as long as I have, Trooper, you'll learn to keep your nose clean."

What he meant about keeping my nose clean wasn't quite clear to me, although I suspected he meant to look the other way. I didn't talk to him long or any time after that. From the conversation there was no doubt in my mind that he was an Uncle Tom. A Tom is worse than a white man in my world because he was two-faced. He could infiltrate the black man's meetings under the cover of darkness, which was his skin color, and then carry information back to the white power structure. In fact, he was more of a parasite who survived solely by preying on others. Many blacks were slaughtered because of this selfish beast of a man.

I spent four months in basic training before I was shipped to Fort Dix, New Jersey, where I spent the remaining twenty months. On December 9, 1954, I was permitted to go home with an honorable discharge. In all, I had done about two years of active duty. I had six more months to spend in the Army Reserves.

I was happy to be going home. The Army had taught me a lot. And the experience of living with all kinds of people had broadened my knowledge of people in general. I learned there were also dumb white people in the world. Before I thought every white person could read and write. Because they had power, it led me to believe that all white people had brains.

Being a soldier in the U.S. Army was actually a very positive experience for my father. And he didn't spend just six more months in the army reserves; he eventually served twenty-eight years.

In 1954, Daddy journeyed back to Greenwood. He could have pursued a considerably easier life in Ohio with his brother Clevester. However, Daddy was drawn back to his home, the rich Mississippi Delta. He missed his family, especially his papa.

Daddy also wanted to become a Mississippi schoolteacher, and now the GI bill would allow this dream to become a reality. The army truly had transformed my father's life, affording him many opportunities he would not otherwise have had.

After getting his G.E.D, Daddy enrolled in Mississippi Vocational College, a Negro college in Itta Bena, which had been built in 1950 for those who were too poor to go to Alcorn College. Daddy was proud to be there. He had a powerful desire to teach colored children. He wanted to help them realize that, in spite of the injustices done to black people, they could become anything they dreamed of becoming. As a child of sharecroppers, he believed that if he could overcome the obstacles, anyone could.

While pursuing his dream, he ran into Arella Love. They had first met each other in the fall of 1952, when Mama's friend Dorothy Mae Cookes introduced them one Saturday night on Johnson Street. It was a brief encounter, but they remained friendly to one another. Actually Daddy was infatuated right from the start. He wrote Mama long letters and sent a picture of himself when he was in the army. When he learned she had married someone else, he stopped writing.

In early 1955 they encountered each other again in front of the Sunshine Cafe. Daddy was a college student by then, and Mama's first marriage had ended. Thus their courtship began. Later, Mama had an opportunity to be on a college campus when she went with Daddy to football games. They also went "clubbing" and on double dates with another couple, Annie Pearl and Michaelroy.

Andrew and Arella were no longer living in different worlds at opposite ends of Leflore County. Their lives had merged.

Black men were not permitted to look at white women too closely. As a result they fell to the wolves for what was called "eyeball rape."

A Lynching in Money, Mississippi

In 1955, about the time Daddy and Mama were courting, a lynching took place in Money, Mississippi, forever altering the lives of blacks and whites in the Delta. People around the world were shocked that something like this could take place, even in the state of Mississippi.

Emmett Till, a fourteen-year-old black boy, and his cousin Curtis Jones were sent from the South Side of Chicago by Emmett's mother to spend a two-week holiday with Till's great-uncle, Moses Wright. Curtis made it safely back to Chicago that summer, but Emmett's unrecognizable body was shipped home in a pine box. Roy Bryant and his half-brother, J. W. Milam, were the accused murderers.

Some blacks believe to this day that there were more whites involved than just those two. Whether there was a mob or only the two infamous brothers is debated, but what is not disputed is that the state of Mississippi did not absolve itself regarding the child's death by rendering a guilty verdict. Bryant and Milam were put on trial and acquitted; they then gave *Look* magazine a detailed description of how they had lynched the boy, apparently being very pleased with themselves. The confessed murderers owned a store in Money, my mother's hometown.

When my mother was a student at Money Vocational High School for Colored Children, she and her friends Natalie and Evelena would cross the railroad tracks to the Milam store, where they would buy candy, pop, chips, a loaf of Wonder Bread, and five cents' worth of "boloney" for sandwiches. Carolyn Bryant, a delicate, young, extraordinarily beautiful white woman, would wait on them.

Many years later, my mother could still recall Carolyn Bryant — and not just because of what happened to Emmett. She said this white woman was the prettiest woman she had ever seen, and most everyone had a difficult time not staring at her. Mama also knew the Wright family; she went to high school with Emmett Till's cousins and uncles. Emmett's great-uncle, Moses Wright, had not known about what occurred earlier on the day of the murder, but he still felt somewhat responsible later.

One of the brothers delivered newspapers to colored people on the Cole plantation. My grandparents were among his customers. "He would drive by in his car, and out the window he would throw a newspaper between two evergreens on each side of the front gate," my mother said, describing J. W. Milam's delivery methods. She went on to tell about what happened after the murder. "When we learned what had happened, Mama jumped up and ran to the door. Mr. Milam was outside in the car about to throw the paper. She was so mad."

Mama recounted my grandmother's reaction to seeing Emmett Till's murderer. "She snatched open the door and yelled, 'We don't want your papers no more.'"

J. W. Milam's reaction was to give my grandmother a hateful stare and yell out a nasty name at her. But he didn't stop at my grandparents' home after that. Many Negroes in the surrounding area immediately stopped doing business with the Milams. Eventually the brothers suffered tremendous financial losses because of what they had done to Emmett Till.

A lot of whites didn't take too kindly to Milam and Bryant either, not necessarily because of the murder but because they had focused the world's eye on Mississippi. Nevertheless, people in the state stood solidly behind the two until after the trial. No white man was going to be convicted of killing a nigger in Mississippi, no matter how barbaric the state appeared to the rest of the world. (When the trial was over, whites called the brothers "white trash." After they lost the store, they had a difficult time finding work.)

Negroes, on the other hand, were roused to action. Throughout Mississippi, blacks were enraged, and a number felt militant enough to join the NAACP. Some historians credit this murder as marking the beginning of the civil rights movement in Mississippi. However, there was fear as well. But it was not the "lie-down-and-pray-to-God-for-a-better-day" kind of fear; it was the "I'm-sick-and-tired-of-being-afraid" kind of fear. Negroes who had children were outraged that white men could kill a young boy over nothing and get away with it.

Since the victim was a black boy from Chicago, the *New York Times* and northern television cameras came to Mississippi. That was the only way in which this crime differed from other murders of blacks, and it didn't affect the outcome. Milam and Bryant were eventually free to go around boasting about the lynching, as other white men had done before. There seemed to be no justice for the Negro in Mississippi, even if the world was watching.

When black Mississippians first heard about the murder on the national news, saw Emmett's bloated body in *Jet* magazine, and read about it in the *New York Times*, they had believed that justice would prevail. They knew about Medgar Evers, Mississippi's NAACP field secretary, and about the Reverend Martin Luther King, Jr., and what he was doing for Negroes in Alabama. Many were inspired. They believed Emmett Till's death would be avenged because, for the first time in Greenwood, white men were being tried for killing a black man. But the brothers went free.

However, even though the trial was a sham, it created an opportunity for Negroes to speak their minds and to vent their anger openly. They didn't whisper in cotton fields and meet in secret. They boldly and angrily glared back at whites who tried to intimidate them. Negro men in isolated areas began to arm themselves, being on the lookout for mobs of cone-headed, white-sheeted men who liked to burn crosses on the lawns of law-abiding black people.

We learned of a black man who was too old to work in the fields and for all the years he had, had nothing to show for it. This man was an Uncle Tom who felt that he owed the white man loyalty or that he would gain certain favors when he stood up, wiggly on his doubtful legs, scratched his cotton-white head and nervously said, "Captain, a colored boy from Chicago was molesting your Missis." It was said that the brother went directly into the store, leaving his fish with another man who had gone fishing with him.

"Who was that boy?" he asked his wife.

"What boy?" She replied with no immediate knowledge of what her husband was talking about.

"That nigger boy today," her husband shouted. "That nigger [a name that he so deservingly earned] told me that a nigger boy had been bothering you." His tone suggested that she might be trying to hide something from him.

70

"What nigger told you what?" she asked, still puzzled by the question.

"That nigger sitting out in front of the store," he spat out vehemently, pulling her to the front entrance of the store.

According to spectators he pointed his finger in the old black man's face. "This nigger." The old man was now scared as he realized this time he had talked too damn much.

The woman explained to him that the boy had only made a wolf-whistle at her, that he hadn't really bothered her. Her husband wasn't satisfied with that explanation. He had to live up to and uphold Mississippi and all southern state traditions.

Before he left the store he asked the old Negro man still sitting in front of the store where the boy lived. The Uncle Tom didn't know where the boy was staying, only that he was from Chicago. Hearing the boy was from Chicago made the white man more furious. He knew black men were mingling with white women in the North.

It was that same evening of terror in 1955 when the Milam brothers found out where the boy was vacationing. Immediately after dark the two brothers went to where Emmett Till was staying with his family. They asked to see the boy. The boy was fetched from his bedroom by his relative and brought into the front room. His murderers were standing there waiting and smiling.

"How would you like to make some money, Boy," Milam asked.

The boy looked at his keeper for an answer.

Milam assured the family by saying, "It'll only take a few minutes. I'll have him back in no time." Emmett was permitted to go, so he got dressed for the last time.

The brothers took the boy to a big barn. They were trying to decide what best to do with him. That night, they used a barn near Money, Mississippi to conceal and perhaps muffle cries and screams of the boy. They stripped Emmett naked and beat him in an effort to exert a confession. The *boy was then taken naked, tied and gagged in the back of a pickup truck. In that truck was a gin wheel. It was to be used as a weight to hold his body on the bottom of the Tallahatchie River.*

After parking, the boy was pulled from the truck, knocked to the ground and pulled up again. The wheel was still waiting in back of the truck. Emmett was told to pick up the gin wheel and carry it to the river bank. Under the weight, he fell to his hands and knees. When he tried to erect himself, he was shot in the forehead. The murderers then tied the gin wheel with hay wire around his neck and deposited him in the river. Three weeks later, not far from Greenwood, a white fisherman found his body.

Meanwhile the brothers claimed that they had let the boy out of the truck not far from his family's house at about ten o'clock that same night. His uncle was no fool; he knew that this kind of thing happened to a lot of Negro men in Mississippi.

When Emmett was pulled out of the river, his body was so mutilated and bloated that he looked like two men. White Mississippi lawyers argued that the boy looked much older than fourteen, as though that made a difference or justified the lynching. Some whites said that it wasn't the boy's body — after the boy's own mother had come from Chicago to identify him. There were still others who claimed that his father had been hanged by the military for raping a German woman during World War II, as though that justified slaughtering the son.

I was a sophomore in college. A bunch of us 'college fellers' attended the trial that lasted for about three weeks every afternoon after class. It was common to see white men other than policemen openly wearing guns in their belts. Black people were not as frightened by this as they would have been a few years ago. The brothers were acquitted on the grounds that there were no witnesses to the murder.

It was the hard work of Medgar Evers and Ruby Hurley which made it possible to have a trial at all, if you call it a trial. By working in the cot-

ton field as field hands, chopping and picking cotton, they were able to find out some information.

One Negro, Willie Reed, heard about the beating of the boy. In fact, he had heard someone screaming that morning, and he knew the brothers. He recalled having been asked to wash some blood from the back of their pickup truck. He said he asked about the blood and Milam told him that he had killed a deer. Reed said he had seen blood of a deer before, and it didn't look like deer blood. He also said it was the hardest blood to clean up. He said it just didn't want to move. When the news was leaked about the boy being lynched, Reed recalled what he witnessed in the Milams' truck and testified to that effect, but the judge ruled an acquittal.

With increasing speed, blacks all over the country were ready to act. There was talk around that blacks from the North were en route to Greenwood. The mayor of Greenwood called out the National Guard consisting of only whites. A carload of all college boys drove pass the courthouse to see if they were really there. They were there, all right, and many blacks in Greenwood were angry for the first time, and Medgar Evers was gaining notice as a civil rights activist throughout Mississippi. Black people everywhere were reading newspapers. I have never seen that many blacks reading the paper in my whole life. I knew something had snapped. Those who couldn't read were being read to by those who could read.

There was a Negro newspaper published every week in Jackson, called 'The Eagle Eye.' This paper told about Mississippi white people in no uncertain terms. We couldn't buy this paper on the streets of Greenwood. My father had it mailed to his church. It cost ten cents a copy. 'The Eagle Eye' sold by the thousands, and Papa couldn't get it fast enough. He would often run out of issues long before he reached half the people wanting them.

My father had begun to stand up for himself. He, like so many blacks, had been pushed too many times into a corner. The talk was: "If we, as blacks, remained humble and frightened, any of us could be killed."

Papa asked, "If they kill a fourteen-year-old boy, what do you think they will do to you or to the rest of us?"

I can only surmise how powerless Daddy and his friends must have felt standing in the colored-only section at the back of the packed courtroom watching Roy Bryant and J. W. Milam being tried for the murder of Emmett Till—a mere boy, an eighth-grader, and the only child of Mamie Till Bradley. This trial was a first for Negroes in Mississippi, so, despite the eventual acquittals, it was a major achievement on the part of Medgar Evers and the NAACP. But the trial also reaffirmed white supremacy in Mississippi. The fact that white men who were not police officers could openly walk around with guns in the courtroom let the world know who was actually in charge.

The message was that, no matter what evidence was uncovered to incriminate the brothers, an acquittal was to be rendered automatically. They had killed a "nigger" who had stepped out of his place regarding a white woman. In the eyes of the twelve white male Tallahatchie County jurors, the two had done nothing morally wrong. In fact, they had done exactly what any one of the jurors themselves might have done. The only controversy was that the rest of the country wanted to tell them how to run things in Mississippi. So, as my father and his friends watched and prayed for justice, the white men sat in that mockery of a trial, laughing and smirking. It was ludicrous to them, all this fuss over the mere killing of a nigger.

Blacks in Mississippi weren't sure about how best to respond to the acquittals. They were angry, but they were also afraid of repercussions. And, although federal marshals were sent to Mississippi to help protect Negroes during the trial, incidents still occurred. For instance, in Glendora, Mississippi, Elmer Kimbrell, a relative of one of the Milam brothers, killed a Negro service station worker named Roy Melton.

It was said that this man provoked an argument by claiming the Negro had wasted gasoline on his car while filling his gas tank. He left the station after an argument with the Negro attendant. Subsequently, he returned with a shotgun. In the dark of night, he sat and waited until the Negro got into his car to leave for home, where his wife and four children were waiting. He never even got his car into gear, when the white man let him have it with both barrels of buckshots from a twelve-gauge shotgun.

The NAACP, headed by Medgar, started right on the case. Again they were able to stir up a trial. This was progress, because before the Till case, to my knowledge there was never before any trial when a white man killed a black. The trial lasted two weeks. The man's only excuse for killing the Negro was that, "My uncles killed a Negro and went free, so I thought I would kill me one, too." There was a furor among blacks when this statement came out. Now white people were on the spot.

Before that they had been able to wash their hands or look the other way and forget it ever happened. But the Till case had attracted too much attention. They were trying to clamp down on white hoodlums, but it was too late. The rumor was that this hoodlum had told them that if they didn't get him off, he would talk — real loud. The man, like his relatives, was acquitted for the murder of a black man.

In this case the so-called good white folks of the White Citizens' Council wanted to do something nice for the slain Negro's wife and children. They agreed to build the family a house. They never did, however. Mysteriously, while en route from Greenwood to her home three miles away in the country, the wife ran into the Yazoo River. Her poor children were saved, but the woman drowned. It was said that the woman was forced off the highway. Someone witnessed the incident while picking cotton. Apparently, the same white man who was tailgating her in his car also dove into the water and saved her children. There was no further investigation, nor was any house ever built.

Incidents like these only made blacks push harder and harder. Still the white men of Mississippi kept up their Klannism. It was not more than ten months later when another black man, Mack Charles Parker, was kidnapped from jail in Poplarville, Mississippi. After he was lynched, his body was thrown into the Pearl River. This black man was accused of raping a white woman who was "in the family way." He was to have a black lawyer, Jesse Brown, represent him. He was going to try and prove that Mack didn't rape that white woman.

Mysteriously, the night before the trial the sheriff conveniently left the keys where Klansmen could get to them, while he stepped out to get a "hot dog." But I don't believe the state of Mississippi could conceive a black lawyer questioning a white woman about a black man molesting her. It had never happened before and they were determined that it would not happen then. They had always taken the white woman's word. This had gone on ever since the 15th century when Negroes were taken off ships in America's docks. As all other cases, no white man was to be convicted for killing a black man. That was an understood fact.

Medgar was not pleased with this kind of thing. In all fairness a lot of whites weren't pleased either. But there was nothing they could do. Many blacks who weren't Uncle Toms were still afraid, although many were not. But still too many were afraid. There was no place to turn. There was no help from the local government and very little help from the federal government.

Whites had a way of doing things in Mississippi, and they weren't inclined to modify their racist practices without being forced to. Thus my father, led first by his father, was attracted to the civil rights activist from the Student Nonviolent Coordinating Committee (SNCC) who came to help organize the blacks in Greenwood.

In December 1955, while the country was still in shock over a senseless murder in Mississippi, my parents married. Before long, they had five little girls.

When I was a little boy, I used to pray to God to make me another color. Not particularly white. I just wanted to be something other than a black boy. A black person was like a snake. It did not make any difference how intelligent or how humble he was. He was still a black man who no one liked. The fact that he was considered a snake is all that was necessary to be killed, lynched, mobbed, or mutilated by any white man or a group of white men who did not like the way a black man worked, walked, spoke, or brushed his teeth.

Five Little Girls

Five Little Girls

All five Jordan girls were brought into the world by seasoned black midwives, who had acquired their medical skills from other black women who had learned the art of birthing from previous generations. Each of us cost fifteen to twenty hard-earned dollars, which was placed in the palm of a skilled practitioner as she went wearily out the back door. No malpractice suits were ever filed because we looked funny or weren't as smart as we should have been. If we looked funny, then that was how God intended us to look, and, since Daddy was studying to become a schoolteacher, there was no excuse for our being dumb. It certainly was not the midwife's fault.

No matter where Mama and Daddy were living, Mama always went "home" to her parents in the country when she was ready to give birth. So, right from the beginning, our tiny lungs were filled with the rich scent of the cotton fields permeating the air of Leflore County. Mama gave birth to each of us on a cotton-stuffed mattress on a four-poster bed in the center bedroom. It was the same bed she had slept in as a girl. Now it was used to bring five little girls into her life and Daddy's.

Thank God, Daddy got girls, because that's all he wanted. Contrary to popular opinion, he was happy every time the midwife told him in a remorseful voice, "It's another girl, Andrew." The reason Daddy was glad was that a black male child's life was too precarious in Mississippi. He knew his own parents hardly worried about his one sister, Viola, but they worried plenty about their four sons. The possibility of a black son swinging on the end of a rope was a realistic one. Daughters were subject to other perils, but the chance of a lynching was remote. It was difficult to teach a black boy how to be a man in Mississippi. My father's own negative self-image as a child weighed heavily on him whenever he considered the possibility of raising a son.

Despite how Daddy had felt as a boy in Mississippi, he was very conscientious about teaching his daughters how to maintain a positive self-image. He never allowed self-criticism from us. And name calling, even in fun, wasn't permitted. We could not refer to ourselves or to one another as ugly, nappy headed, or big lipped. We were told right from the beginning that we were beautiful, and that is how we were taught to feel about ourselves.

Bernice, the eldest and tallest sister, was born in 1954. I was born in 1956 and was named Rosa Marylon. (Many years later, after I married, I changed my name to Jordana, a derivative of our family name.) I look like Mama because of my high cheekbones. I cherish the stories of how Daddy was so "crazy" about me when I was born that he spoiled me rotten. It seems that I wanted to be held and rocked a lot. Daddy was in college at the time, so he and I spent many late hours together rocking and studying for exams. Perhaps I wasn't too fretful and he actually got some studying done. Of course, I don't recall any of this; I just remember that from an early age I adored my father.

Mary Ella, who has Mama's nose, came next in 1957. Velma Lee, the redheaded baby who looks like Aunt Viola, was born in 1958. Evone, the youngest and smallest baby, was born in 1959. Mary and Evone look the most like Daddy.

Technically, my oldest sister Bernice is from my mother's first marriage, but Daddy is the only father she has ever known. Whenever Daddy was asked how many children he had, he would answer without hesitation, "I have five girls." Therefore, Bernice is the firstborn of the Jordan girls, and our lives began in Mississippi.

I used to watch my sister powder her face. She would always buy white powder. She would put layers on her face in her attempt to look lighter-skinned. After walking the dusty country roads to Sunday School, in the middle of the day she would sweat. Her face would look like a fish pool where water scarcely covered the surface. The cheap powder would roll up like bread dough, creating an impression of wear and tear due to old age. I used to kid her a lot about the excessive use of the powder. We would often get into some heated arguments and as a result I was usually chased out of the house with a butcher knife.

We loved Daddy's stories and all other stories told to us by the black folks who helped shape our lives in Mississippi. We were surrounded by people who enriched us in various ways. They were interesting and spiritual people who told us endless tales — sad, funny, and heartbreaking ones about struggles to survive. We were surrounded by grandparents, aunts, uncles, and cousins, and also by people we didn't know very well, except that they were our elders. I refer to them collectively as the "Mississippi

Village." Our family of seven was large by any standard but became enormous when all the people who had a say in our upbringing, directly or indirectly, were included. Of course, our
parents influenced our lives the most.

When we were growing up we never heard the African proverb
"It takes an entire village to raise a child." What we understood
as children in Mississippi, nearly three decades before Hillary
Rodham Clinton wrote *It Takes a Village*, was that a whole lot of
folks were involved in our upbringing, whether we liked it or
not. And we had better never sass one or show disrespect in any
way. Ultimately, we had to tolerate all kinds of colored folks,
including those who chewed tobacco, dipped snuff, or were
grouchy, nosy, or mean-spirited, relatives or not. This meant
that if Miss Lizzie Bell or Ol' Bro Fate said to stop whatever it
was we were doing, then we were wise to quit. Naturally, if they
told Mama, Daddy, or one of our grandparents that we hadn't
paid them any mind, that we kept right on running through the
flower bed or climbing the pecan tree, then we were likely to
get a real good "whupping" once we got home. The rule was that
if a grown-up said something like, "Y'all chillins betta stop doin'
that right now," then we had to stop that minute.

My sister Mary Ella made a grave mistake one summer. She
was playing out in the street, and Mrs. Harris, the very old lady
who lived in a dingy white house one row up from ours, hollered
off her porch, "Stop that, Mary Ella. Get out of that street."

Paying her no mind, Mary kept right on darting on and off the
curb. She even picked up some rocks and threw them at the old
lady's porch. We were about four and five years old at the time. I
was sitting on the grass laughing my silly head off. We were in

our shorts. It was a hot summer day and soon to become a memorable one.

My laughing is probably what prompted Mary to cross the line further. I can't speculate how else she got it into her head to pat her butt at the old lady. Mary turned her behind around so that Mrs. Harris could get a real good look. Stooping way over, with her left hand on her left knee, Mary patted her behind with her right hand. She did this in Mrs. Harris's direction three or four times. Hysterical, I fell over on my side and squealed with laughter. It was amazing that I found my sister so funny. She was defying a major rule of our upbringing, but at the time it seemed hilarious.

Well, that old lady didn't say one word. She just reached for her walking stick, slipped open the screen door, and made ready to come off the porch. I didn't remember ever having seen her off the porch before that day. Certainly, she must have come out of that house, but I had never seen her do so. I knew only that she always manned her post behind the enclosed screened-in porch. Her Majesty came out that summer, though. Mary saw her, too. We watched together, and neither of us was amused by then. I was no longer laughing, and Mary was through entertaining the neighborhood. Old Lady Harris was coming out of the house, and she was not looking at either of us. Mary and I didn't know what to expect, and we were petrified.

Mrs. Harris steadied herself on the three brick steps that led to the sidewalk in front of her house. She held her knobby walking stick in one hand, and the other one, gnarled and bony, tightly gripped a silver guard rail. She inched her way down, taking one step at a time until she had reached the sidewalk. It seemed to go on forever. Mary and I could have escaped to Ethiopia during the time she took. We wondered where she was headed—was she coming to get us? I worried that she might kill my sister by beating her bloody with that old ugly cane. We didn't know enough to run for our lives.

Hunched over, Mrs. Harris was small and frail in her pink floral cotton housedress, a faded garment that closed with white snaps. She wore practical black lace-up shoes with thick support hosiery knotted at the top of her swollen arthritic knees. With much determination, slowly but surely, she made her way down the path to our little house. From the window in the kitchen where she was washing dishes, Mama could see Mrs. Harris coming. Mary and I peeked around the side of the house. With an apprehensive but welcoming smile, Mama opened the front door before the old lady could knock. It was Mrs. Harris's first and last visit to our house.

Mary and I waited around the side of the house for what seemed like an eternity. We were scared to death. I didn't know how much trouble I was in, but I feared Mary was in way over her four-year-old head. We crept around to the back of the house and sat side by side like two chain gang fugitives.

"Rosa, Mary Ella, y'all get in here, right now."

When our names were called, we jumped to our feet. Mama sounded angry. Mrs. Harris, looking very pleased with herself, was making her way back up to her watch post of a porch. She seemed to have a little satisfied bounce in her steps as she turned back up the path.

When we got in the house, we had to ease carefully past Mama's hands, which seemed to want to snatch an unruly child's arm. She asked us what we had been doing. Feeling somewhat like a

snitch, I told Mama I hadn't been doing anything except playing. Mary said the same. Being her buddy, I didn't refute her. I
looked everywhere other than at Mary or Mama. Finally, I settled
my shifting eyes on the faded blue linoleum of our squeaky clean
kitchen floor. Then Mama smiled at us and cocked her head. I
wasn't fooled for a second. I knew she had neither lost her mind
nor forgotten her parental duties. She said to Mary, "Mary Ella,
Mrs. Harris said you were playing in the street, and that you
threw rocks at her house. And when she told you to stop, you
patted your butt at her. Did you do that, Mary?"

Mary shook her head and began to cry. Mama told her not to
cry, just to tell the truth. Mary got the hiccups and began to
stutter. I didn't say one word. Then Mama got really clever. She
said to Mary in a joking kind of voice, "Now show Mama how
you patted your behind at Mrs. Harris."

Before Mary could respond, Mama proceeded to lean over in
her summer print and pat her narrow hips, doing it with a lot of
bouncing, exaggerating her movements. It was more like hips
going up and down, as her slender hand tapped a beat. Mama
was willowy so she didn't have much of a butt anyway, whereas
Mary was short and chunky, with a plump little behind.

"Did you do it like this, Mary?" Mama asked, bouncing and
swaying her behind for emphasis, as she patted it a couple more
times.

Mary began to laugh, because Mama was being so comical.
My other sisters also were laughing. I don't remember laughing,
though I may have smiled. I would like to believe that I wasn't
that gullible. Mama's antics were obviously a setup. And since
Daddy was at the army reserves for the weekend, his lap would
not be available as a source of consolation.

To my horror, Mary jumped up from the floor, wiped her eyes, and said, "No, Mama, I did it like this."

Mary showed Mama and the rest of us how she had patted her butt at Mrs. Harris. She did it exactly as she had done earlier. Everyone was tickled to death. Mama also laughed, and, to make certain she had the right image, Mama asked Mary to demonstrate again. Mary did her little show again and again, becoming an expert butt patter after so many demonstrations. When we had settled down, Mama gave her some sobering instructions. She told Mary to go outside and get a switch off the bushes. The look on Mary's face should have been framed. The rest of us girls got really quiet. Mary had broken a cardinal rule by being disrespectful to an adult. She was pitiful to watch, sobbing miserably as she went from bush to bush, searching fruitlessly for what she would not find — a painless switch.

Something else we weren't allowed to do was to interrupt "grown folks' conversations." If one of us girls even appeared to be about to butt in, we would get a look. Mama was really good at this, especially when she was talking with another mother. This was not only to keep us in line but also to let the other colored women know that she had her five girls under strict control. Back then colored people wouldn't just call the unruly child "fass" if a girl or "mannish" if a boy; they would bad-mouth the mother as well. They would make remarks such as "You know, she don't have no control over them chillins of herrrns. They is just as wild as heeethens."

Mama was always conscious of the fact that bad behavior from any of us would reflect poorly on her. The look she gave us was all it took. However, if what we had to tattle was really important to us, we would endure that look and wait for an opening.

We would have to sit around quietly and see whether she was inclined to stop and acknowledge our existence. Mama was very good at this also. She could treat you as if you belonged to her and at the same time as if you weren't really there.

Children back then knew how to hang around discreetly, being seen and not heard. If you got into trouble everybody knew who your family was. Mothers especially seemed able to sense if their child was the guilty party, even if they looked busy or were engaged in grown-up interactions. Suddenly, out of nowhere, a mother's hand would appear and snatch a startled child, catching him or her in the act. Some kids knew their mothers pretty well, or they had been caught often enough so that they were always on guard. These kids were constantly looking around while they played and did their mischief. Their parents had to rely heavily on the "Mississippi Village" to keep them informed.

If we really wanted to be acknowledged, we didn't dare look Mama or whomever she was talking to dead in the face; that could be deemed disrespectful or considered an attempt to listen in on "grown folks' conversations." Back then children didn't listen actively; grown-ups knew we really were listening, but out of respect we pretended that we weren't.

Colored folks in those days were not advocates of children's rights. Fortunately for us Jordan girls, we were fairly well behaved so we didn't get into trouble too often. Mama made certain before we left home that we wouldn't embarrass her in any way. She would line us up by the door and repeat the rules: "No running through other people's houses; take a seat. Do not talk too loudly. If the other kids are playing outside, do not go in and out. Absolutely no begging. And, of course, don't interrupt grown folks' conversations." Mama took pride in all the compliments she got about our good behavior. Imagine, five girls seen and not heard.

I learned that grown-ups could be very ornery and that they liked letting you know they were superior. They acted a lot like they said white folks did. They were also telepathic. They knew when the house was really on fire, as opposed to when a kid was just itching to tattle (in which case you were in for a long wait). Sometimes you would forget the crime you had wanted to report on, or you would be so nervous that you could hardly get it out. When you finally were acknowledged, more than likely you would get a it-had-better-be-worth-this-interruption look. That alone could make you tongue-tied. "Umm Maarrrrieee wonnnn't llettt mmeeee plllllay wwiiiith heeer."

The outcome was usually not worth it, especially when you got yelled at for being a tattler within earshot of the perpetrator. Unless Mama or the designated in-charge grown-up actually saw or heard the offense with her own eyes, then you were in a lose-lose situation all the way around. We girls learned quickly that we were better off solving our own squabbles in lose-a-few, win-a-few unspoken agreements.

When Daddy was around, he would use a let's-sit-down-and-try-to-resolve-this-issue approach. He took great pleasure in practicing his schoolteacher training on us. This didn't work to our satisfaction either. We girls found that Daddy could lecture at length, and playtime was too valuable. It was best to work it out ourselves and keep right on playing.

Our uncle Will, one of Daddy's older brothers, lived with Grandmama and Granddaddy Jordan. He was rather quiet. He and Daddy got along well. It was said that he was "wrapped too tight" and could be dangerous if provoked. We girls didn't mess around with him much, although on occasion he would give us a nickel. I attempted to converse with him a few times. He mostly mumbled, but he was always smiling. I thought he was shy, not crazy. He watched us play all the time. I figured if Daddy liked him, he couldn't be all that crazy.

Aunt Viola was the nicest aunt that any kid could ask for. She would brag and rave about us and make us feel really special. When she introduced us to her colleagues it would be with much fanfare. We enjoyed going to her house, and we liked her hearty, laughing husband, Uncle Roosevelt. She called him "Doc" because he had a Ph.D. Aunt Viola's hair was naturally red back then, and she wore it short and curly. She couldn't have children. Mama said she had had stillborn twins, and I believe she had several miscarriages.

Our next-to-youngest sister, Velma (the "knee-baby" is how Daddy referred to her status in the birthing line), took after Aunt Viola in appearance. She was named after our grandmother in the country, although Evone, the youngest, really looks more like Grandmama. Velma has never liked being told she looks like Aunt Viola, although Aunt Viola was a beautiful woman in her younger days, as Velma is today.

Though Greenwood was small, as children we seldom got to play with our cousins. Uncle David is married to Aunt Chris, and their kids are the only Jordan cousins that we know about. Little David, the oldest, had beautiful white teeth and was the friendliest in the whole family. He made us feel especially welcome with his joking and carrying on. Darrell and Donald, the younger boys, didn't have their older brother's friendly personality, so we never got to know them well at all.

But I do remember when Uncle David contracted tuberculosis. We went to the hospital to visit him. His nickname for Daddy was "Head," which irritated us girls no end. We thought it was a put-down, although Daddy always laughed. He didn't seem to mind it in the least.

Bernice especially enjoyed going over to our cousins' house, because she liked playing around with David. Cousin Joyce, the only girl in their family, is a year older than I am. Besides the Jordan name, she and I didn't have much in common when we were kids. Everybody compared us a lot. I was supposed to be the "prettiest," Joyce the "smartest." At any rate, I was said to be the smartest among the Jordan girls. My sisters, of course, would contest that statement, and I wouldn't blame any one of them. At times the "Mississippi Village" stirred up a lot of mess by comparing the Jordan sisters.

Early on as a child growing up in Mississippi, I became aware of segregation, realizing as time went on that this was why I had so little contact with white kids. I wasn't supposed to be around them and they weren't supposed to be around me. Most whites in Mississippi didn't want colored kids like my sisters and me going to school with white kids. My father wanted to change all that, even when he himself was still a student in college and we were just babies.

I was standing on Highway 82 trying to thumb a ride to Greenwood from college. I wasn't thumbing white people, just black people, because I didn't fully trust whites. I stood for only a half hour before a black 1956 Imperial stopped in front of me.

"Get in, Boy," he said. "Do you go to college?"

"Yes, Sir," I said.

Then I attempted to get in the back seat, which was customary in the South. He insisted I sit up front with him, so I did. After he started for Greenwood he asked me another question.

"Can I talk to you man-to-man?" I assured him he could.

His question was whether I was in favor of integration. He made reference to public schools. I hesitated momentarily, trying to figure out what kind of an answer I should give him. That is, whether I should tell him the truth or say what he wanted me to say.

I collected my thoughts and said, "Yes."

"Yes, what?" he asked for clarification, looking at the highway and at me fifty-fifty.

"I'm in favor of integration at any level," I told him nervously.

"Why?" He asked, appearing not to be disturbed at all. At least for a while he wasn't.

"I'm an ex-GI, Sir. I have lived with all kinds of men. This experience has renewed my thoughts and beliefs in people. I worked in the Army with all kinds, and I have seen people working well together for the most part. So, I don't see why it cannot work here in Mississippi."

After I finished talking, he said, "I'm in favor of integration up to a point."

"What point, Sir?" I asked this, becoming aware that the car was slowing up. He continued.

"I'm in favor of it on the college level, but not on the elementary level."

He explained to me that, if children grew up together, there would be less of a chance that the values about racial purity could be instilled. He went on to say that definitely he did not want a Negro having intercourse with his daughter. I told him that the decision to become involved, socially or intimately, should be left up to the two people in question and not the establishment.

I could see the conversation was getting to be too much for him, because his face had begun turning bright red, and a purplish color flushed the neck of his open-collared white shirt. But his discomfort couldn't be helped; he had asked me my opinion and on a man-to-man level.

When we came to a turn which was not in the direction of Greenwood, he stopped the car and said that was as far as he was going. I vacated the car and thanked him for the ride. He then made a left turn toward Itta Bena, about five miles from where he had given me a ride. I resumed my thumbing and walking and thumbing. As I walked in the ninety-degree heat in the dead of summer, all kinds of things ran through my mind — like, why didn't I lie to him and ride home? Then I suddenly realized that I couldn't lie about a thing like that, although many blacks lied about their feelings just to make things temporarily a little easier for themselves.

My father was incapable of going along with Mississippi's educational program, which crippled black children academically. He felt strongly that black children and white children should attend school together and that it was time to discontinue such practices as having black children receive worn, outdated books in separate and unequal schools. He realized that his own inferior education had been a hindrance to him; he had had to work very hard to overcome his own deficiencies while earning a teacher's certificate.

He believed that it would be horrendous for another generation to have to suffer through a backward educational system, the proponents of which didn't care whether black children amounted to anything more than maids and porters. I know my father had very high aspirations for us. Because of his beliefs he would rather walk in the sweltering heat than keep company with a white man who was worried about maintaining racial purity and a racist agenda that would keep black girls and boys relegated to inferior status. Daddy would rather walk through hell's fire than let things continue as they were in Mississippi. When he became a teacher, he was determined to change things so that his daughters could obtain a better education than the one he had received as a child.

The few white people I observed worked in department stores in downtown Greenwood or were cashiers at the Liberty Cash grocery store. I recall hearing my maternal grandmother—but never my parents—answering "yes, ma'am" and "yes, sir" to white people who were much younger than she was. I, too, had a problem with this when I got a little older. And, as my father had done when he was a kid, I asked my grandmother why. Giving a response similar to the one my father had received, she said that that was the way it was in Mississippi.

So, despite the determination of black men to fight for their rights, whites in Mississippi were adamant in their belief that they were superior to blacks. This pervasive attitude infuriated my father. Whenever he was confronted by whites who took great pleasure in attempting to rub black faces in the malignancy of white supremacy, further resentment would fester within him. On several occasions when he and my mother interacted with white store clerks, they had to deal with racist attitudes.

My mother told the story of shopping one day in Kantan Men's Store. "We were looking for pants for Andrew," she said. "A white man came over to us smiling nice and big. Then he asked, 'Boy, gal, what can I do for y'all today?' I said to myself, 'Oh, here we go again.'"

Mama looked at Daddy's rigid face and became a little uneasy. She knew Daddy was not going to fall in line. He would never succumb to playing the part of a nigger.

"Andrew didn't even look at the man. He just kept on looking over the racks. I tried a smile, then I told the clerk we'd call him when we had made a decision. But the man ignored me and went over on the other side of Andrew. This time he said, 'Boy, what can I help you with?' He wasn't smiling and his voice was louder and firmer. He was becoming agitated because he probably thought he was being nice when he acknowledged us when we first walked into the store."

(This is typical of how some whites dealt with "new blacks" during the civil rights era. Store owners knew they could be financially ruined if blacks boycotted, so they smiled, placated the customers, and didn't let them wait too long. But they continued to refer to black men and women as "boy" and "gal" instead of "sir" and "ma'am.")

"Andrew looked right through that white man," Mama continued. "Then he handed the man the pants he had selected and moved past him to the counter. That white man was so startled that he took a couple steps backwards. He couldn't believe what he was witnessing. I quickly followed Andrew to the counter. We really couldn't afford the pants Andrew had chosen, but it was worth every penny we paid. The way Andrew handled that situation made us feel like dignitaries. We walked out of there with our heads held high, and that cracker found out who the 'boy' was, and it wasn't Andrew."

On that occasion, my father was able to maintain his composure; however, in other situations when white clerks would insist on a "yes, sir" or "no, sir" reply, Daddy would continue to deliberately say "yes" and "no" with a very professional tone and demeanor. Many white clerks, not appreciating his "arrogance," would walk away without serving him. Under these circumstances, Daddy was happy to take his business elsewhere. He just had too much pride.

It was difficult for me to keep a job because I couldn't lie and scratch my head when talking to a white person. I couldn't smile when he wanted me to, or respond when he called me Boy, Sam, Willie, Blue or all other names that Southern whites cooked up for blacks. I had to be frank with them whenever an issue was presented to me, even though it would always mean my job.

My grandmother was self-employed, but when I was a child it seemed to me that she uttered "yes, sir" and "yes, ma'am" every chance she got—even when it didn't appear that the white person cared one way or the other. I believed she was intimidated by whites and had become so conditioned to "being in her place" that she was overly cautious and too solicitous.

As I've gotten older, I have realized something else about the situation. My grandmother was living a very good life and probably didn't want to call attention to how well she and Grand-daddy were doing with their country store. She didn't want to appear to be "uppity actin'." The truth is, they had more money than the average white family did in Mississippi. From their point of view, it was perhaps best not to rock the boat.

What really confused me as a little girl was what my own people wanted us to call ourselves. I heard "Negro," and that was deemed proper—I think. But "colored"? What did being "colored" mean? Did it mean that we were supposed to be white but had been colored, as with crayons? Or did it mean that we had been dipped in various shades from white to deep blue-black and were therefore "colored"? Did that mean we were supposed to have been white and by some quirk or accident we had changed color? I had no idea what being "colored" meant or why this term was preferred by some over "Negro."

In Mississippi, I believe Daddy preferred "Negro," although he could switch back and forth, depending upon the person with whom he was conversing. The more educated the person was, the more likely he was to use "Negro," I think. But this is still not clear to me. In Mississippi, as in South Africa, light-skinned blacks were called "colored," and darker-skinned blacks were called "Negroes" sometimes, but not always, because educated light-skinned blacks referred to themselves as "Negroes" as well. As a kid I was confused by all this no end.

It wasn't until we moved north that I heard the reference "black" being used as a positive term for my people. This was in the late 1960s, when the black power movement took Negroes and colored people by storm. We became "black and proud of it." The next term was "Afro-American," which I thought indicated that we had big hair and were full of soul and hip-hop. Before all of this new racial awareness, during the days of my childhood in Mississippi, the term "black" was considered derogatory. It meant that your skin was too dark and was ugly. "She's soooooo black" was said in the nastiest way. On hot summer days, instead of being allowed to play, black kids were called into the house, usually by a grandparent, so they wouldn't get "too black." And lighter-skinned people were considered to be more appealing to the opposite sex. References to skin color seemed to be an obsession for black people.

Because of the negative connotations, when "black" became fashionable, many continued to refer to themselves as "colored." I still occasionally hear an elderly person say "colored" instead of "black" or "African American."

Ironically, to be called "African" *anything* back then was hurtful. It was an offensive and demeaning charge, an insinuation that you were less than human—ignorant, uncultured, dark-skinned, and ape-like. It meant that your features, such as big lips or a wide nose, were too African-looking and were less than beautiful, even if you were light-skinned. Someone who referred to you as an African American when I was a kid was trying to hurt your feelings.

Hair texture was also a big issue. The straighter the hair the better. If you were blessed in having naturally "good" hair or hair that looked like white people's, then you were something special. To have light skin and "good" hair made you the cream of the black crop. Of course, a hairdresser with some Royal Crown hair grease and a hot straightening comb could do a superb job with kinky hair. And those who really disliked their dark complexion could try Dr. Fred Palmer's skin whitener as a remedy.

There was nothing confusing about the "white only" and "colored only" signs on public facilities, however. "White only" meant just that, and was not intended to include any shade of black whatsoever. "Colored only" signs referred to all black people, Negro, colored, whatever you called yourself; that was where you went. Sometimes, though, the wording was not so clear.

The signs that hung in public places, signaling white and black with arrows pointing in opposite directions, were understandable because if you were white or black you could not go in the door which did not bear out your complexion. But the doors that read 'gentlemen' and 'men,' or 'ladies' and 'women,' were confusing. I was never quite sure who was a gentleman, or who was a lady, although I had an idea what whites meant. 'Men' were for blacks, and 'gentlemen' were for whites, and likewise 'ladies' and 'women' for white and black women, respectively.

Apparently, growing up as a black child has had confusing aspects for several generations. Having a schoolteacher father helped tremendously, because he could explain the changing times, at least as much as he himself could keep up with. Black people have gone through a lot of changes in becoming comfortable with our racial identity, and historical racism in this country is the root of the problem.

When Daddy was a college student, he was an activist for civil rights, and was once expelled for a semester from the Mississippi Vocational College. He was outspoken on campus and unwilling to wait for the racial climate to improve in Mississippi. He had witnessed what could happen to black men, whether they were passive or willing to stand up. He believed that if death was the end result for black men anyway, they were better off fighting the oppressor; they could not all be lynched.

During the civil rights movement, Daddy's progress as a man and as a father was rapid. By birthright, a white man was entitled to be both, whereas blacks had to fight for their rights as men in the United States. Following his father's example, Daddy had begun to stand up for his manhood.

My father was not a coward. He proved that many times when someone tried to misuse us. However, he was hampered by the environment that engulfed everything around him. But it was for the love for his family that he took so much and worked so hard for nothing.

Daddy's parents lived on Avenue H in Greenwood. He and Mama stayed there for a little while when they first got married. The Jordans' rented frame house was green and rather square-shaped with white trim along the roof. The toilet was precariously situated on a small porch attached to the rear of the house. At the front of the house, during the summer, family and friends gathered on a large porch for conversations that were punctuated by hands thrown up to greet neighbors who rode or walked past. This all-black section of Greenwood was populated by folks with various kinds of professions and employment.

The only ways to determine whether someone in the neighborhood was middle class or well-to-do were to find out if he owned his house or to see how well furnished it was. For instance, Mr. Morgan, an insurance agent who owned houses in other black areas, lived across the street from my grandparents in a well-dressed big house. Mr. Moe, a brickmason, lived in a nice house on Avenue H, as did a barbershop owner, a tailor shop owner, a shoeshine shop owner, and a schoolteacher (my father).

In Greenwood, if you were black it didn't matter who you were, where you were employed, or what you could afford; you lived in the section designated for blacks. Of course, the majority of blacks were poor anyway. But unlike whites who prospered and moved to the suburbs or to wealthy areas like those along River Road, blacks could not rent or obtain a mortgage outside of black neighborhoods.

But although the Jordan family was still poor and struggling, things were looking up and the future was encouraging. My grandparents' sparsely furnished but sturdy house was a great improvement over the shack they had lived in on the Charles Whitington plantation. Daddy's sister, Viola, had graduated from Southern University in Baton Rouge, Louisiana, and was teaching school in Greenwood. Uncle David was a student at Mississippi Vocational College. So there were to be three schoolteachers from the Jordan household. Much of the credit belongs to my grandfather.

"Daddy Jordan was always preaching that education was the key to integration," my mother said. "He said, 'When the doors open up you have to be there to take advantage of the opportunities.'" When our family moved into a shotgun house in an alley behind my grandparents, Daddy was still in school. Granddaddy Jordan would habitually stop by our house to see how we were getting along.

"Daddy Jordan would come around to the house," Mama explained. "If Andrew was home, he would ask, 'Boy, why aren't you at school?' Andrew would tell him, 'Papa, school is out today.'"

Mama said that Daddy would say this with a big sigh. It seems my grandfather was relentless in his mission to push his children to improve themselves.

My mother liked her in-laws very much. Unlike her own mother, who was very stern, Grandmama Jordan was easy to laugh and joke with. Grandmama Jordan, a diabetic, worked for years as a maid at the Malouf Hotel. Many days she was too sick to work, but she went anyway, and was cheerful and optimistic, never a complainer.

Grandmama Jordan was sickly when I was a kid, and her eyesight was not very sharp. Mama said she had sugar diabetes, or just plain "sugar," as she called it. Now, "sugar" to a six-year-old meant white, grainy sweet stuff, and I imagined it coursing through a person's body. No wonder my grandmother didn't feel well, I thought; I didn't feel so good when I ate too many sweets either. Grandmama Jordan, according to my childhood logic, shouldn't have eaten all that sugar.

Since her eyesight was not very keen, she would ask me to thread needles for her. This task was carried out on her front porch unless it was raining, in which case it was done by the light of a window in her mostly green house on Avenue H, the only place I remember her living. She sat on a green glider on the front porch to do most of her sewing. She would sway, sing, and hum her favorite hymns to the squeaking of the glider and the passing of cars. She could sing "Amazing Grace" very nicely.

Sitting beside Grandmama on that glider made threading the needle very difficult. I couldn't keep my hands steady long enough to meet the eye of the needle. Eventually, I would sit on the porch rail until I could fulfill my duty.

Grandmama Jordan, always patient and smiling, would keep right on sewing and humming church hymns. Her thimble finger would push the needle through a flower pattern until I had the next color ready. I was nervous about my assignment, because, although she was patient, the task always seemed to take longer than I thought it should. To this day, whenever I see a thimble, I think of her.

But it was Granddaddy Jordan who was the head of the family. After moving into town, he became quite different; he was no longer the sharecropper father explaining to his son why he had to say "yes, sir" to a white boy. And, long before the civil rights movement, he was an activist among Negroes in Greenwood.

At sixty years of age, Cleveland Jordan was a devout Christian still going to the National Baptist Convention as a representative of the Zion Baptist Church, as he had done for many years. However, he wasn't willing to just pray that things would change for the younger generation. Nor was he willing to leave the finding of solutions up to his more educated peers, many of whom he considered to be Uncle Toms. Granddaddy was a leader in his own right. In fact, during the 1950s he helped organize a voters' education movement. He himself was a registered voter long before it was fashionable.

When he was a member of the Citizens League, an organization created as an alternative to the less intimidating NAACP, he was a mover and a shaker, wanting to get things rolling. He soon became unhappy with the passivity of the organization. He believed that if black people were going to have a better life in Mississippi, it would be because of men who had the determination to stand up and the fortitude to relentlessly confront racist institutions. Although a deacon, he didn't take too kindly to any ministers who he felt were spineless and unsupportive of the progress of the movement, disparagingly referring to them as "grip toters and chicken eaters." Granddaddy Jordan gravitated toward young black activists, and he stuck his neck out for them on more than one occasion.

Granddaddy Jordan during the Struggle

The first active members of the SNCC (Student Nonviolent Coordinating Committee) to reach Greenwood in 1962 were Willie Peacock and Samuel Block. The day they arrived they made the age-old mistake of talking to the wrong Negroes. Because of that they were almost killed the first night in town while sleeping in a room they had rented from a Tom. In the middle of the night, they had to escape down a television pole. Making their escape from the Klansmen, they tried to seek refuge in other black homes. But these folks, fearing for their own safety, refused them. After some three or four houses they arrived at our house. My father welcomed the two, and I was proud of him.

Within a few months, more members of the SNCC began to pour into Greenwood and all over Mississippi, but particularly in Greenwood. They came in large numbers and spread across Mississippi. The movement had begun, and fear mounted from day to day among blacks as well as whites. Many Negroes, the upper middle class — Uncle Toms in particular — complained that the young people didn't have any morals and they were not sufficiently trained to lead them. Yet none of them professed to have the correct morals and training, and not one of them was willing to stand up and be counted. The meetings were being held at the Elks Hall because no minister was brave enough to allow a meeting in their church.

As the movement continued, and with my father's constant pounding on them, the doors of the churches eventually swung open. Papa would say whenever he spoke at a mass meeting, "If the preacher cannot lead, he will not be fed." The crowd would go wild. They all agreed with him.

The Negroes in Greenwood were afraid to be seen talking with members of the SNCC, and eventually the Freedom Riders as well. They were afraid of losing their jobs, especially those who were schoolteachers, principals and other middle class blacks. In some cases, Negro maids were so afraid of losing their positions that they would come to the mass meetings in order to report back to their bosses, just so they could stabilize their situations.

We called them "Nervous Nellies." In many cases they were the first ones fired.

Greenwood's population was approximately thirty thousand. About sixteen thousand of these were black people, and approximately fourteen thousand were white. Out of the sixteen thousand blacks, there were only five hundred registered voters. Many blacks tried to register, but didn't have the two dollars for the poll tax that was a requirement for black voters. And some did not wish to wait the six months to one year before they could vote, provided they could at that time present a receipt indicating that they had paid the poll tax. Jim Crow Laws were playing havoc with our lives in Mississippi.

Those who registered or attempted to register found their names placed in the local papers so that their bosses could see them. In order to keep their jobs, many were told to withdraw their names from the Voters' Registration books. If they refused, they were fired and couldn't get another job in Mississippi. Those who did withdraw their names were permitted to keep their jobs, and those who were fired were often intimidated. Sometimes they were beaten, and in other parts of Mississippi they were slaughtered.

The white man had miscalculated the black man as he has always done, although thirty years ago it might have driven Negroes into a state of quietude. But no more. It made things worse. The more blacks died, the more blacks became aroused. And since there were no plantations to keep poor Negroes occupied, he had nothing. He couldn't even grow a garden, raise a hog, or have a milk cow. All of that was taken away from him. He was hungry and maltreated, so he wasn't willing to be oppressed and starved too.

It was spring of 1962. Reverend Donald L. Tucker, a young Methodist minister, was sent to pastor a local A. M. E. Church on Walthall Street. It was the second church to accept the movement. The first one had been First Christian Church pastored by the Reverend Aaron Johnson, the first minister in Greenwood to open his church to the mass meeting.

However, Reverend Tucker had a dynamic force over his members, and he was young and inspiring. His followers trusted him and were willing to follow him even to death if need be. We knew that he was our best chance among the ministers.

Mass meetings were held at his church almost every night and, as the movement progressed, people came by the hundreds. Local speakers were heard before guests such as Dick Gregory, Medgar Evers and others. My father would always start the meeting off. He had a motivating voice, but in a joking kind of way. But what he said was never taken as a joke. He made people laugh, but they knew he was serious. It was the way he talked or how he said it. Papa was not educated, and he didn't know correct English, but he knew the Bible, and the way he spoke was all that was necessary to get the ball rolling.

After Papa had his say, the students of the SNCC would start off with the freedom song of the movement, "We Shall Overcome." Only two or three voices would be heard until the whole audience joined in. We would sing for fifteen or twenty minutes until all the additions to the song were exhausted; then young Reverend Tucker would rise and speak.

My grandfather was extremely dedicated to the success of the movement. In fact, the initial mass meetings in Greenwood were held at the Elks Hall because Granddaddy Jordan was a member, and he was able to secure this place. Ministers were petrified after the 1955 murder of the Reverend George Lee, president of the Belzoni chapter of the NAACP. The Reverend Lee had received numerous death threats, and one night his tire was blown out and the lower half of his jaw blown off. His death was ruled a traffic accident. My father and grandfather went to his funeral.

Reverend Lee's fate was sufficient reason to deter Negro ministers in Greenwood. They weren't predisposed to taking risks, and being killed was a real possibility. But Granddaddy Jordan was insistent and even insulting. He felt that the movement and the young people needed the support of black churches if things were going to change. So, as a lay minister, he offered his allegiance when the ministers did not.

When the "new blacks" came to Greenwood to challenge the status quo, it wasn't easy for blacks to open their doors to strangers who could potentially bring harm to them and their families. Although blacks were angry and wanted to take action, they didn't want activists staying in their homes. It was one thing to have a meeting, but if an activist was reported coming and going from a home, those who lived there might lose their jobs, or the house might be bombed. Few were willing to take the risk. Often these young men had to sleep in abandoned cars or travel to other towns for the night.

Granddaddy Jordan took on an enormous responsibility when he offered refuge to Samuel Block and Willie Peacock. Eventually, the problem was solved when the two stayed only a short time at each of several homes, thereby minimizing the risk for each family by making it difficult for the white power structure to track the men down.

This wasn't the first time Granddaddy Jordan had helped Samuel Block. Block had first arrived in Greenwood alone, sent by Bob Moses, director of SNCC. The organization had received a grant to establish a Voter Education Project in six counties in Mississippi, and Leflore County was one of them.

My mother told me that when Block initially arrived in Greenwood, he roomed with Mrs. McNease, the black principal of the elementary school. Mrs. McNease had no idea what he was up to when she rented him a room. Then Block pretended to be a student at Mississippi Vocational School while he perused the neighborhood for recruits. When he attempted to organize meetings at the local churches, he was met with extensive resistance. Talking to my grandfather, Block learned about Greenwood's history, including which blacks he could trust.

Only a few blacks attended the first mass meeting, held at the Elks Hall. Granddaddy Jordan introduced young Block to the congregation and asked the people to support him and to treat him like family. He told them that courageous young people like Block were essential if the movement was to survive. After this the people became more receptive and were eager to learn the freedom songs. Block taught them the words to "We Shall Overcome" and "I Ain't Scared of Your Jails," and this helped them to feel inspired.

The mayor of the city was soon tense. The Elks, under pressure, refused to allow the meetings to continue, and Block was forced to look elsewhere. Soon Mrs. McNease began to receive threatening phone calls, and she asked him to leave her house. With my grandfather's help, Block was able to convince the Reverend Aaron Johnson, minister of the First Christian Church, to open his doors to the meetings. The Reverend Donald Tucker was able to make an even greater impact.

Soon Block was taking people down to the courthouse so that they could register to vote. Although they went, they weren't getting registered. The infamous Martha Lamb, dragon lady registrar, was there to block them. Police Chief Curtis Lary was on guard as well, taking names to be placed in the newspaper. He was also there to prevent his crazed officer/Klansman, Captain Usser, from busting the heads of too many Negroes. Usser, one of the more disturbed officers, had an affinity for kicking and bloodying the heads of would-be registrants. Nevertheless, going down and attempting to register was a significant step for Negroes who had always before been intimidated.

My grandfather's convictions and belief in the movement helped to keep Daddy from being stuck in a passive role. The time had come for schoolteachers to take a stand. Unfortunately, in Greenwood, Daddy stood alone with a big family to support.

As I rose from the bench my legs stiffened and my tongue clung to the base of my mouth.

On May 13, 1960, Daddy graduated with a bachelor of science degree from Mississippi Vocational College (now known as Mississippi Valley State University). James H. White, the first president and one of the founding fathers, signed his diploma. The day should have been one of the happiest in Daddy's life. However, he had not had the opportunity to become a traditional student. He had started college in his mid-twenties, then married and soon had a big family. He did not have a carefree student's life. He worked, studied, and was a father.

Preparing himself to become a high school business teacher had been an incredible feat. He had become proficient in the teaching of typing, shorthand, accounting, and other related subjects in his field. He was going to make an excellent teacher. He was a young black man who had accomplished his goals in spite of humble beginnings. This achievement was bound to be an inspiration to his students. He certainly was an inspiration to his family. However, becoming an educated man had also brought out the militancy in Daddy. The more he learned, the less he was willing to be subjected to.

When I was a young girl, Daddy was gone a lot. Mama explained that Daddy got home late in the evenings because he

113

was teaching in neighboring towns outside of Greenwood. One school year he was so far away that he could come home only on the weekends. Daddy's involvement in the civil rights movement also kept him out late at night. It was usually long past our bedtime when he arrived at home.

At any rate, Mama said it was very hard on her, Daddy being gone so much, especially when she was pregnant or had two of us in diapers. She knew Daddy was doing the best he could to keep food on the table and a roof over our heads. Mama also said we moved quite a bit, but mostly within a fifty-mile radius of Greenwood so Daddy could be home at night. I remember living in Tupelo and Hattiesburg. Permanent teaching positions were not plentiful, so Daddy went wherever there was an opening, even if it was just for one school year. Sometimes we stayed with my grandparents when things got really tough (my mother's parents mostly, as they had the financial wherewithal to take in six — or, counting Daddy, seven — mouths to feed).

When we lived in Hattiesburg, Mama was especially happy because Daddy was able to help her care for us. Daddy was a fairly new schoolteacher in his late twenties. Our family rented a small, raggedy, shotgun house. If you opened the front and the back doors, you could see straight out to the patchy grass in the backyard. A porch supported by four cylinder blocks offered a direct look underneath the house. There was not much furniture. My parents' bedroom was in the front. My sisters and I slept in the other bedroom, which had two big beds on either side; Mary Ella, the middle child, usually slept with Velma and Evone, and Bernice and I occupied the other bed. Run-down though it was, for at least nine months the place was home to us. We were all together, and Daddy was home at night. That's what mattered most to me.

I can remember that house particularly well because it was where my sisters and I got the measles. In a one-week period, we were all struck down by a rash and fever. We ended up lying in bed like the five little bears. Daddy came home early each evening, and I looked forward to seeing him. My sisters did, too. His big hand covering our foreheads, checking for signs of a fever, always brought a smile to our crusty, sore lips. He smiled sympathetically while administering his fatherly medicine.

Both my parents were loving and attentive. Sometimes we would get on Mama's nerves when we ran through the house, but in those years she was with us all the time.

Daddy didn't get a permanent contract, so we lived in Hattiesburg for just one school year. Some time toward the end of that year, Daddy took Bernice and me to school with him. It was a beautiful balmy day, with a slight breeze. It must have been May Day, because I remember a pole with pink and blue ribbons streaming down the length of it. Boys and girls were singing a song as they went around the pole, going in and out as they held onto a ribbon. They were all dressed up, the girls wearing dresses and ribbons in their hair and the boys in Sunday suits. At that time May Day was celebrated in schools and at church picnics.

I had on a pretty pink dress and shiny patent leather shoes, but I was told by a teacher that I was too young to go around the pole. I wasn't too happy about this. Bernice, dressed in a fluffy yellow dress with a springy underskirt, got to go around that colorfully disguised tetherball pole. It didn't look so difficult to me; all they did was go in and out and around. Bernice took hold of the pink ribbon and sang the little May Day song, strutting in and out with the other "big kids," primly ignoring me. It wasn't in the least bit fair.

Bernice, being rather tall for her age, also got to race with the other kids in a relay event. She borrowed a pair of tennis shoes and entered the race. But this time I didn't allow anyone to inform me that I was too young, not even Daddy. When the whistle blew I was right with those other Negro kids, sprinting for all I was worth across a grassy field in my black patent leathers. I heard Daddy yelling for me to come back, but I kept right on running as fast as I could.

I finished last, way last, then burst into humiliating tears. Daddy came out to retrieve me. He was laughing hard; so were the other teachers and the kids who saw me trying to win that race. He grabbed my hand, wiped my face with his handkerchief, and took me, sniveling, over to the sidelines. He told me that I had done a good job, which made me feel somewhat better. Bernice, however, earned a third place ribbon. She was disgusted that I had cried. I was very proud of her, though. At least one of the Jordan girls had earned something for her effort. And Daddy was proud of both of us.

By 1962, Daddy was finally a middle-class professional and could provide sufficiently for his family. He should have been very proud of himself. However, as the civil rights struggle continued in Greenwood, he had to sit passively during the mass meetings, not voicing his outrage, which caused him to feel like a coward.

Daddy believed that "schoolteachers and ministers should be leaders." He felt that he was letting black people down by not taking his turn at the helm of the civil rights struggle in his hometown. In spite of the fact that he was the only school-teacher in Greenwood attending the meetings, rarely missing one, he wanted to become more active. Although realizing that he was responsible for a large family, he didn't feel fulfilled.

It was now fall, and I was teaching school in Greenville, a town 54 miles from Greenwood. My dream of teaching had been long fulfilled. However, I wasn't happy. I wanted to do something for my people. After all, that truly is what getting an education is all about. To just teach school was not enough, especially under the conditions blacks were being subjected to in Mississippi.

It took some time in the beginning for Samuel Block and Willie Peacock, the young leaders of the SNCC, to arouse enough blacks to have a mass meeting. At the first meeting there were only about twenty people. Block talked first, then Peacock. They didn't get very far with the older people. Some were afraid. The younger people who were there spoke out. I just sat quietly. I couldn't participate because I was teaching in a public school and if the superintendent knew I was there I could lose my job. I had a wife and five children to support. Those were the thoughts passing through my head. I was no different from those frightened Negroes mentioned above.

The next night there was another mass meeting. The crowd was less that night than the night before. The meeting adjourned at eleven-thirty. I went home hating myself for my cowardice. The fear of losing my job had power over me. I could think only of my own welfare and that of my family. There were people who were less fortunate than I was, who were taking risks. I had an education and yet I was a coward. I could get a job anywhere. There were blacks who were poor with no education and no place to go. I felt like a fool. I knew I had to get involved. I have always wanted to do something for my people, and now the time had come. Yet, I was too much of a coward to answer the call. That thought haunted me all that night.

The next morning I was still haunted by the cowardliness that had possessed my soul. I got up early that morning without awakening my wife. I drove to school, my mind preoccupied with thoughts about the movement. All that day I was not myself. My students must have detected a different attitude. Perhaps, unconsciously, I had transplanted my lack of manhood into my classroom.

Three o'clock didn't come soon enough that day. I was out of the building within seconds of the dismissal bell. I jumped into my car and drove as fast as I could. I had driven only twenty miles when I was pulled over by a highway patrolman. When I stopped, the patrolman rushed up to my car with his pistol in hand.

"Get out of that car, you black son of a bitch," he said backing up just enough for the door to swing open.

"Put your hands up, nigger," he ordered, while patting me down with his left hand.

Then he pushed me against the car while still holding the pistol in his right hand. With his left hand, he called the police station for additional policemen. Two plain-clothed policemen came within minutes. They were told to take me downtown to Indianola. I was ordered into the car. I sat in back of the car, unhandcuffed, while the two plainclothesmen sat in front. The one on the right asked for my driver's license. I asked whether he was a policeman. He said, "yes." Then I requested some kind of identification, his badge. The one who was driving remarked: "What difference does it make, nigger, whether we are policeman or not?" He said this while looking at me through the rear view mirror.

"I'm not supposed to submit my license to anyone except an officer of the law, Sir."

I said this with my hands and eyes concentrating on the king-sized Coke bottle lying on the floor of the car beneath my feet.

"Yes, we are police," said the one on the right, presenting me his badge at the same time. I looked at it closely before saying, "Thank you, Sir."

After about five minutes we were at the city jail.

"Hey, Willie, I've got another one for you," said the policeman who was driving.

Willie was a Negro trustee. He was a huge man standing about six-eight. He pulled me from the car like I was a common criminal. After pushing me up three flights of stairs I reached the cell where I was to spend four wasteful hours. The cell was exactly eight-by-eight with a ceiling measuring not more than eight feet high. Six men already occupied it. I made seven.

We hardly had space to move. In the middle of the floor was a ten-gallon tub of water. It was the water we were supposed to drink. Directly across the tub of water was a toilet. I was denied a telephone call, so I asked for a piece of paper. Willie, the trustee, refused to give me any paper. Another Negro, also a trustee, brought me a notebook. I had a pencil.

He gave it to me and said, "You can write it, but the judge is gone fishing and won't be back until six o'clock this evening."

I completed the message and gave it to him. At six-thirty the judge had Willie bring me to his office. Willie did it grudgingly. When Willie had assisted me through the door the judge said, "Okay, Willie, you can go now."

Then jokingly he said to me, "My God, you've had a little trouble?"

Politely I said, "Yes, Sir, I have."

"Well, you can go now. The fine is nineteen dollars — fifteen dollars for the fine and four dollars for room and board."

I started to protest because I hadn't eaten anything or slept. The four dollars just wasn't justified. Thinking better of it, I decided to keep my mouth shut.

"By the way, boy, what is all this?" he asked with a dumbfounded expression. He held up a handful of test papers from a shorthand test that I had given my class. He may have thought I was associated with the Communist Party. His expression changed almost completely when I told him I was a high school teacher a few miles from his town. He put the papers back into my briefcase.

"They said you weren't drinking."

I assured him that I didn't drink or smoke.

"Well, the fine is still nineteen dollars," he declared the second time.

"Sir, I don't have any money," I pleaded. "I won't have any money until the end of the month. We get paid only once a month," I explained further.

As a schoolteacher I was making three hundred and thirty dollars a month. It was then the twenty-eighth day.

The judge permitted me to leave with the assurance that he would have me picked up if I didn't pay him as promised. I paid him, all right. I wanted no part of that jail again. It was worse than a dungeon.

I arrived home about seven-thirty that night. I told Arella what happened as I rushed through my dinner. I wanted to make the next mass meeting. When I arrived at the meeting, Samuel Block was talking to a small group of people. That night, small gathering that it was, there were more people there than usual, mostly people who didn't have jobs or food to eat. Because they had nothing to lose, they wanted to march and try to register to vote. Unlike most of the so-called decent people, they weren't afraid. They had only their lives to lose.

After Block finished speaking he said to the audience, "We have a brave schoolteacher here. Stand up, Mr. Jordan," said Block, his pearly white teeth fully exposed.

"This is Mr. Andrew L. Jordan. He has been to every meeting."

He then asked me, as I was still sitting, "Mr. Jordan, do you have anything you want to say to these people?"

Top: Andrew Lee Jordan, Greenwood, Mississippi, 1963 /
Bottom: Rosa Jordan (Jordana Shakoor), Toledo, Ohio, 1966

Top: Hamp Love, Lilly (William Love's second wife), and Velma Love,
Greenwood, Mississippi, 1970s / Bottom left: Cleveland Jordan, Greenwood,
Mississippi, 1950s / Bottom right: Arella Love, Money, Mississippi, 1955

SCHOOL DAYS 1962-63
STONE ST. ELEM.

Top: Clevester Jordan, Toledo, Ohio, 1950s / Bottom left: Viola Sission, Greenwood, Mississippi, 1962 / Bottom right: Elizabeth Tate Jordan, Greenwood, Mississippi, 1950s

Top: Clevester Jordan (left) and two unknown soldiers in World War II, 1940s /
Bottom (left to right): Evone, Mary, Rosa, Velma, and Bernice, McClinton Nunn
Homes, Toledo, Ohio, 1965

Top: Andrew Jordan (center) with students, Spencer Sharples High School, Toledo, Ohio, 1973 / Bottom: Arella Jordan, Spencer Sharples High School, Toledo, Ohio, 1973

Top: Andrew Jordan holding Ali Shakoor (first grandchild), 1974 / Bottom:
Andrew Jordan and Keyomah Shakoor (granddaughter), Columbus, Ohio, 1988

Top: Andrew Jordan and Ali Shakoor, 1990 / Bottom (left to right): Cousins Daryl and Joyce, Aunt Chris, and Uncle David Jordan, March 1991

Top: Andrew L. Jordan, May 21, 1931-March 15, 1991 /
Bottom: Jordana Y. Shakoor, 1996

I rose from the bench that seemed to have magnetized my body and walked to the front of the building so that I was facing the audience.

"I am happy to be here," I said. "You all have shown courage in coming. You have exhibited the kind of concern for your welfare that every black man in this country should have shown many years ago. With people like you willing to protest and to try to vote, the movement has to be a success. I will do whatever is demanded of me to see that you get what is rightfully yours."

I then took my seat. The group applauded me for what seemed like a full minute. I felt good all over. I had gained compulsion and I knew I had to go through with it. When the meeting was over I stayed around and talked personally with almost every person in the building.

I believed leaders should be ministers and teachers, because they come in contact with more people than anyone else and more people will follow them because of their leadership ability. A minister is not paid by the white man — he is paid solely by his membership, and therefore he should not be entirely afraid. On the other hand, a teacher should not stick his head out too far, unless he has the majority of the teachers with him. In my situation, the blacks at the meeting admired my willingness to help, but they were afraid that I was putting my career in jeopardy. I assured them that I was aware of all repercussions and was willing to endure any form of intimidation that might be cast upon me by the white power structure.

It was twelve-thirty when I got home. My wife, Arella, was displeased.

"Where have you been, Andrew?" she asked with tearful eyes.

"I was at the mass meeting," I told her, then kissed her on her high cheek bones.

"What are you into now?" She said this in a complaining voice. "You know what happened the last time," she reminded me.

Arella was talking about the strike I led at Mississippi Valley State College in 1957. I was one of the first to be put out of college and I had no *job. I was going to school on the GI Bill, and when I was not in school, I didn't get the hundred and sixty dollars a month stipend. My involvement in the protest and subsequent expulsion caused my wife and family — three girls at that time — to live with her parents, and I with mine, for six months. I knew she was worried that I might lose my job. I was worried as well, but I was committed.*

For almost a year, Daddy managed to be instrumental in the mass meetings without jeopardizing his teaching career. This was largely because his father, Reverend Tucker, Sam Block, and Willie Peacock strongly discouraged him from marching out in .the open. They felt he had too many mouths to feed. During this phase Daddy gave some very moving speeches and felt somewhat placated by doing so. The movement was gaining significant speed in Greenwood.

Blacks in other parts of Mississippi, especially in Jackson, were boycotting stores and having a tremendous financial impact on white businesses. At last blacks were realizing that there was strength in numbers. Those who refused to stop patronizing white businesses found themselves at the receiving end of black militancy, although, when a Molotov cocktail soared through the night into someone's living room, the attack was attributed to Klansmen. Soon blacks in Mississippi were in sync. The movement was progressing rapidly. Daddy was excited. It was time to become more open about his involvement in the struggle, in order to recruit other schoolteachers.

One night in March of 1963, before our march to the courthouse, the Reverend Tucker called the movement to action. In retrospect, he sounded much like the Reverend Martin Luther King, Jr., our great leader who was making a name for himself as a great civil rights leader in Alabama.

He said, "Ladies and gentlemen, we have a job to do. God has given us the power and the know how; now it is up to us to use it wisely. Yes, some of us will suffer, and some of us will go hungry or perhaps die. But nevertheless, if this is truly our mission, we must be willing to stand fast against whatever the task may be. I am prepared. How many of you here will follow me to the courthouse tomorrow? May I see some hands?"

Many hands flew into the air. Reverend Tucker was pleased.

"Meet me here at ten o'clock tomorrow," he told the crowd.

When he sat down, black people near him extended their hands of approval and congratulated him for taking a stand. Papa got up and let out a yell. He was happy.

"I will walk by your side, Reverend," he told Reverend Tucker.

Papa had registered to vote years ago — before a large number of blacks had even thought about it. White folks didn't particularly worry about the five hundred or so black voters that Papa was one of, because they still had the balance of power. But when blacks attempted to register by the thousands, they knew things would change. When the meeting was over almost everyone in the church rushed to the front to shake Papa's and Reverend Tucker's hands.

The next morning I went to school. I was now teaching in Tchula about thirty miles from Greenwood. I was asked not to march because there were too many other people who were not schoolteachers. The belief was that they didn't have anything to lose except their lives.

The next morning the group met at church on time. They were briefed on how to march and on what to expect. Then they lined themselves up in pairs of two's and proceeded towards the courthouse.

They reached the courthouse about five blocks away at exactly 11:00 a.m. There waiting for them was a group of policemen with billy clubs. At first they did not try to interfere with the marchers. Not just yet. They allowed them to enter the courthouse. The clerk, Martha Lamb, refused to

123

allow them to register. The marchers then turned without a word and walked back out of the courthouse onto the lawn. There they sang and prayed for a while, then they started back to the church down Main Street. The Reverend Tucker, my father, and another Negro called "Freedom" led the way. Freedom had earned that name because he had participated in marches from coast to coast. I never knew his real name.

When they reached the No. 5 Station on Main Street a car filled with policemen pulled up in front of the marchers and stopped. Two policemen armed with clubs and dogs jumped out of the car and ordered the group to stop marching and to disperse. Reverend Tucker raised his hand, signaling the group to stop. The marchers stopped.

Then he asked the marchers, "What do you want to do? Do you want to march and sing or break up?" He asked this in a soul-stirring voice.

The marchers replied, "We want to march and sing."

Two hundred people had voiced their opinion. The march proceeded about ten more yards, before a brutal policeman turned the dog on Reverend Tucker. The big brown police dog, a German Shepherd, leaped for his neck, but fell short and landed in his chest, knocking Tucker to the street. Black folks said, "Like a big grizzly bear, the dog stood over Tucker growling, daring him to move."

"Kill the son of a bitch," shouted the policeman, with tobacco juice spraying all around him.

Papa knocked the dog away from Tucker with his fist until the policeman got him under control. Then he stooped and lifted Tucker from the pavement all by himself because there was no one to help. The panicked group of marchers had fled in a hundred directions. Papa carried Reverend Tucker to a car driven by a Negro, which drove them to Dr. Burns' office. The dog had managed to plunge his teeth into the young Reverend's leg, tearing away human flesh.

Uncle Tom ministers took great delight in learning that the Reverend Tucker had been attacked. They were quick to call him a fool. They felt that he should have waited for them, although they showed no signs of taking a stand.

Medgar heard about the SNCC being in Greenwood and the attack on Reverend Tucker. He came quickly to find out what the NAACP could do. We said, "Set up a chapter of the NAACP in Greenwood." Medgar attempted to explain what had happened before. He was talking about the branch we had in Greenwood a few years back that did not survive. We assured him that it would be different this time.

Medgar agreed by saying. "I'll call the national office tonight, then I'll let you know later."

We passed out pamphlets letting people know a mass meeting was being held to discuss our having a NAACP chapter. A week later people turned out in large numbers. The church could not hold all of them. There were microphones set up on the outside of the church so everyone would know what was going on. The meeting opened with "We Shall Overcome," then "I Want My Freedom." There were verses added to the song each time the song went around.

We had a good half-hour for singing freedom songs before Papa got up to speak.

"I am sixty years old," he said. "I have lived in Mississippi all of my life, and I have lived around Greenwood for forty years."

Then he paused.

"I saw a terrible thing happen the other day."

He paused again.

"I saw a white policeman sic a dog on a black preacher and called him an SOB. I will never get over that."

Papa was very upset. He went on with much emotion. "God didn't call no black SOB to preach. God called a man. The policeman said the dog didn't attack Reverend Tucker."

He went on to explain. "I was talking with Reverend Tucker when that dog attacked him. I knocked the dog off him, and I carried him to the doctor. If anybody said that dog didn't bite him, he's telling a damned lie."

When Papa realized he had cursed he quickly turned to Reverend Tucker and Medgar Evers who was there for support.

"Forgive me, gentlemen, I didn't mean to curse."

Then he sat down, tears flowing. Papa dabbed his eyes with his big black-and-white polka dot handkerchief. He was very emotional.

After the request was made for an NAACP chapter in Greenwood, Medgar Evers personally asked Daddy, Granddaddy Jordan, and the Reverend Tucker to be the organizers.

Old-timers like my grandfather, Richard West, Henry Sias, C. C. Bryant, Louis Redd, and Amzie Moore, as well as those like Landy McNair and Ida Holland who had also gone to Reverend Tucker's aid on that decisive day, were courageous people who were willing to risk their lives and livelihoods so that Negro children of the future would not become second-class citizens. Because of their perseverance and effectiveness, young people like Samuel Block and Willie Peacock were able to make immense gains in the Greenwood civil rights movement.

In April, a meeting was called. Medgar Evers was there. The church was packed like a sardine can. Spirits were elevated, and devotion and determination were immeasurably high. The usual thing took place. My father would open the meeting, then there would be singing and praying. Reverend Tucker, aroused by the singing, rose and made a few remarks. Then Medgar Evers went to the podium with his reddish-color hair shining in the light. He made this profound speech to the Negroes of Greenwood:

"Ladies and gentlemen, I have come tonight to help you become first-class citizens. It has been requested of me by you to set up a branch of the NAACP here in Greenwood. This means that you must support the local if it is to exist. The national office is pleased to have you as members and

as Freedom Fighters. As you know we have a great struggle in the state of Mississippi and in this country, but particularly in Mississippi. We will win eventually, but we will not get any help from other people until we try to help ourselves first.

"I will not stand before you and say that it is not risky; for I know too well that it is. There have been many of us who are leaders who have been shot, lynched and only God knows what else, but that has not stopped the movement. The movement must not stop. If we stop now we might as well cut our own throats. We Jacksonians are boycotting now. A boycott is as effective as you make it. Saying you will boycott is one thing, but really boycotting is something else. I hope you get the message. I have one other thing to say. As of now you have a chapter in the greatest organization in the world and born here tonight, the Greenwood Chapter of the NAACP. You must now elect your officers. Thank you for lending me your time."

When Medgar sat down, the crowd stood and hailed him for five minutes. Then there was the election of officers. The first to be elected was Reverend Tucker for president. The second to be elected was I, as executive secretary of the National Association for the Advancement of Colored People, Leflore County, Mississippi. The other officers were elected as needed. But, first a careful screening of the men took place to make sure they would stand up under fire or pressure.

The official meeting under the new chapter of the NAACP was able to get fifty members the first night of the organization. Blacks joined the organization proudly. Many had waited for years to join, but did not know how or whom to contact. There was also fear that they would speak to the wrong person and get exposed to the power structure. We assured them that only the local branch and the national office knew of their membership and neither of us would or could publicize it. Only a member could reveal his membership to someone else.

We asked them not to carry membership cards in their wallets because if they were arrested the policeman would see it, which may subject them to undue hardships unnecessarily. Many said they could care less about the police or the power structure knowing they were members of the NAACP. They said they would carry their membership cards proudly.

Yes, some were arrested and beaten for having a membership card, and the cards were taken and ripped to pieces. But that didn't stop the movement. It only magnified their desire to become members. There were those who went to chop and pick cotton for two dollars a day in order to join. These Negroes numbered about a hundred. There were those who couldn't walk or were too sick, who made phone calls to the office for someone to come by their house so they could join. Still there were those who were simply afraid to be seen entering the office, who made requests for someone to come to them so they could join.

The young people desired separate recognition. They wanted to become junior members. These youth proved to be the backbone of the meetings. They had guts, were motivated and were willing to push. If they were frightened, they had their parents as backup.

We renewed our boycott efforts with greater commitment than ever before. The burning of Negro property and churches were now actual acts against the movement, and this was enough to get some of the die-hards off their behinds. If they had no other reason they were now forced to act. In Greenwood we were able to close many stores that did not comply with Negroes. The boycott had worked and for the first time in the history of Mississippi, and throughout the entire South, black people knew their strength. This gave blacks more courage to fight and to push the country for what is promised to all men in the constitution. With President John F. Kennedy in the White House, we believed we would succeed in obtaining full citizenship during the 1960s.

Accepting the position as secretary of the Greenwood NAACP chapter gave Daddy tremendous responsibilities and brought upon him enormous risks. There was a lot of work to be instituted. Recruiting new members and issuing membership cards were Daddy's responsibilities. Further, he was required to take the minutes at the mass meetings and send a report to Medgar Evers at the state headquarters in Jackson. This time the chapter could not founder. Residents of black Greenwood had to show their willingness to support the organization if it was going to survive and be taken seriously. Medgar Evers was counting on those who took office to keep things going and to give him a full accounting. So, between taking part in these activities and grading papers and preparing for his classes, Daddy was overwhelmed.

"Andrew was never home," Mama proclaims about that year. When Daddy got home from school he would rush through his dinner and be out the door to the mass meetings. When he was home he was always doing paperwork, either for his classes or for the NAACP, and people were constantly in and out of the house, coming to get their memberships or planning the next meeting. Mama said we never had much time to ourselves until Sundays.

During this period our family was living in a four-room house in an alley near Avenue H. We were still right behind Daddy's parents. Naturally, being this close eased the pressures on Mama because Grandmama Jordan was a big help with us girls. But if things became too stressful, she would send Bernice and me to stay with our grandparents in the country. We'd stay for a weekend or, in the summer, for a couple of weeks.

The proximity to his parents benefited Daddy as well. Granddaddy Jordan kept him informed while he was teaching school, and they could attend the meetings together in the evenings. When they wanted to talk about black folks and the situation in Mississippi, they would sit on the front porch of my grandparents' house, on the squeaky green-and-white glider. My sisters and I would play on the steps or run up and down the sidewalk. Mama would be in the kitchen talking with Grandmama Jordan.

Together, father and son would develop strategies for the next mass meeting. It was obvious how close Daddy was to his family. When he spoke to his parents he was very respectful and used a soft tone. When Daddy said "Mama" or "Papa," his voice was like velvet. He and Granddaddy Jordan had a common mission, and they always seemed to be in collusion.

The few times Mama and Daddy took us to mass meetings, my sisters and I would come back singing "We Shall Overcome." Our grandparents on both sides got a kick out of that. We went to church together on Sundays, but not as often as we should have. Mama and Daddy were just too tired—besides, a lot of gospel singing, preaching, and praying went on at the mass meetings.

Though Daddy was gone a lot, when he was home he helped around the house. And he was a good father, one who changed diapers in the middle of the night. He played with us girls and took turns holding our dolls when we wanted to play house. Daddy patiently taught us how to read, do arithmetic, and tell time. He was constantly correcting our grammar. Of course, any kind of game with our schoolteacher father was a teaching moment for him, even checkers.

According to Mama, Daddy also did most of the grocery shopping and was inclined to wash dishes. I remember him making the creamiest mashed potatoes, which I think he learned how to do in the army. He could also make a jelly cake from scratch.

He simply was not home often enough to do a lot more. However, his absences were what made my childhood experiences with him so precious and memorable to me.

Mama does not discount the risk of Daddy's involvement in the struggle. It was understood between them that the Greenwood civil rights movement needed every black family to support it. Black women had to give up a lot. They knew that black men had been killed throughout the South, that jobs had been lost and businesses destroyed. Daddy and his father had attended several funerals of blacks who were murdered by whites. He and Mama both had driven by the burnt remains of Mr. Brown's Cleaners.

Mr. Brown and his wife had moved to Greenwood from nearby Minter City, and had opened a dry cleaning business on the corner of Avenue H. Because of his activities in the civil rights movement, a Molotov cocktail was thrown into his establishment. This happened the same night — March 24, 1963 — that the SNCC office in Greenwood was gutted by fire. My parents realized that the risks were great.

One rumor circulating in Mississippi was that Medgar Evers would be assassinated. Who else was on the list was anyone's guess. It was understood that any black man involved in the movement could become a potential target.

"Yes, I have to say at times I was scared," declared Mama. "Especially when Andrew would come home really late at night. Some of those white folks in Mississippi were crazy. And they were dirty about how they did things. They didn't care if you had a family or not. But I also knew that Andrew had to do this. Andrew was not the kind of man who could sit back and not do his part. He was miserable when he restricted himself. He acted like he felt like less of a man." She said she had to support Daddy in his decision.

When Daddy was working with the civil rights movement, he didn't pound it into us girls that black people were being discriminated against. I don't believe he wanted us to feel hurt or resentful. Daddy was angry enough about the situation for all of us. But it wasn't to be our battle; we were to be little girls, sheltered and insulated from all the ugliness around us. We did attend some of the mass meetings when he was speaking. But Daddy didn't preach hatred, either at home or in his speeches, no matter how frustrated he became with the progress of the movement.

My parents never taught us to be prejudiced. We came to understand as we grew older that white people thought that black people were inferior. We learned through osmosis that black people were fighting for equal rights, and that was why Daddy was gone a lot.

Daddy was driven to make a difference in Mississippi for his children and for the black children of the future in the United States of America. In Greenwood, before 1965, Daddy stood as the lone schoolteacher, willing to make whatever sacrifice was required.

He would later lose his career. Medgar Evers would soon lose his life.

We hoped somehow, by some authority or force of power, that justice would be rendered for the brutal and inhuman ambush of Medgar Evers.

The Death of a Leader

It doesn't matter how forewarned people are: when a leader is felled, there is a profound effect on the survivors. Medgar Evers had many survivors in addition to his wife, Myrlie, his three children, his brother, Charles, and other family members. Thousands of black people in Mississippi and throughout the country were devastated when they learned he had been slain.

Born in Decatur, Mississippi, in 1926, Medgar Evers was the forerunner of the civil rights movement in the Magnolia State. A World War II veteran, he challenged the racist system in 1946, when he and five other young veterans, including his brother, went down to the courthouse to register to vote. They were to be the first Negroes in Decatur to become registered voters; fewer than 5 percent of black Mississippians throughout the entire state were registered. Whites in Decatur were buzzing like hornets. "How dare those Evers brothers bring that nigger mess to Decatur" was probably said all over town.

Later that year, when election time came, they marched to the courthouse to cast their ballots. They were met by about thirty armed white men blocking their way to the clerk's office. Some of the angry white bigots were people the black men had known when they were boys. An uneven parallel line was formed, and six would-be Negro voters were denied their constitutional rights.

Medgar and the other black veterans found themselves in confrontation not with German or Japanese soldiers but with white men in their own hometown. However, Medgar thought it best that day to hold his temper. Whites in Decatur had a history of being vicious toward blacks who rebelled against the status quo. If the six men pressed the issue, they might end up beaten or shot down in the wee hours of the morning.

Like my father, Medgar went to college on the GI bill. He attended Alcorn College, where he met his future wife and partner, Myrlie Beasley, who was from Vicksburg.

By 1952, Medgar was deeply involved in the NAACP. He had become a member shortly after he had tried to vote in Decatur. It seems the Negro man with the reddish coloring had found his calling, and was making a name for himself as someone who had courage and conviction. Soon he was busy organizing chapters among small farmers and sharecroppers in the Delta. By 1954, Medgar was the NAACP's first field secretary in Mississippi. He served as a liaison between the state and national headquarters. He was responsible for recruiting new members and for investigating racial harassment and lynching. Additionally, he encouraged Negroes to register to vote.

Medgar was willing to travel wherever he was needed; he could be counted upon day or night. He helped Negroes find other employment when they lost their jobs as a result of trying to register. If lives were threatened or homes were firebombed, he got funds from the NAACP to aid Negroes in relocating to other states.

In Mississippi, Medgar Evers was relentless in his fight for equality and for the betterment of black people. He was thirty-seven years old when he died, and he was my father's idol.

The death of Medgar Evers deeply affected my father. Daddy admired Medgar's courage and his tireless efforts to challenge the injustices blacks suffered in Mississippi. They shared the opinion that teachers and ministers should be leaders; on several occasions, Medgar had said how disappointed he was in those who were unwilling to stand up. He criticized teachers for not being openly supportive of the civil rights movement. He challenged ministers who did not open their doors to the mass meetings. He took both groups to task for discouraging disenfranchised blacks through their own lack of involvement in the NAACP.

Teachers were a serious bone of contention for Medgar, because Negro teachers in Mississippi had benefited the most from the NAACP's initiatives to equalize teachers' wages. In essence, teachers had gone from making poverty wages to having middle-class status. So, instead of being paid twenty dollars a month, Negro teachers were making up to five thousand dollars a year by the 1950s. Medgar believed that, because of this, Mississippi teachers should have become visible civil rights leaders in their communities and advocates of the NAACP.

Therefore, when Medgar personally asked Daddy for his assistance in restarting the Greenwood NAACP chapter, my father would have died rather than let down this great American. When Daddy accepted the position as secretary of the chapter, he not only was serving his people but was also honoring Medgar Evers, a man he felt had sacrificed tremendously to make life better for black people.

The KKK, publicly known as the White Citizens' Council, had been rumored to be plotting Medgar Evers' assassination. A Negro who worked at the Greyhound Bus Station in Greenwood testified some months later that he had overheard a murderous plot on the night before the ambush shooting of Medgar. But at the time he didn't know whom they were talking about.

That night Beckwith, who worked sometimes as a human traffic director, making certain that blacks and whites went into designated rest rooms, was having a discussion with a white woman. The Negro stated that the white woman got up and said, "I'll kill the black son of a bitch." But the man who patrolled the bus station, Beckwith, quickly rejected her. The bus station worker said that Beckwith said he would do it, and it was agreed that he would. Later that evening Beckwith called a meeting at the bus station. This all took place on June 11, 1963.

On the next night, June 12, mass meetings were being held in Jackson and in Greenwood. Medgar was attending his own meeting, while we were attending ours. In Jackson the meeting was being conducted at the Masonic Temple on Lynch Street.

A white man was noticed walking around the outside of the temple, looking up at the office window. Although he was noticed, nothing about him seemed suspicious, because there were other whites there as well. Some were reporters and some were sympathizers. A few minutes hence, the man came into the office of the NAACP. It was the same man who was looking from the street below. He was asked if he wished to take out a membership. He refused and walked out quickly, according to bystanders. Shortly afterward he was seen talking to a policeman in Jackson, in front of the temple. Then he was seen getting into a car across the street. A Negro named Whitehead had driven the car from Greenwood to Jackson.

Whitehead testified to the local chapter of the NAACP and to the SNCC in Greenwood, while Reverend Tucker and I listened some eighteen months later. He said he had been given fifty dollars by Beckwith to drive the car to Jackson, but he didn't know why he was driving there.

Medgar's meeting adjourned at eleven-thirty. He left for home feeling depressed, following a bad week of mass meetings. When his car pulled in the driveway, a man was concealed behind some honeysuckles with a 30-30 rifle. Tired and defenseless, Medgar was shot in the back as he reached for the screen door that opened to his kitchen.

Like all civil rights workers in Mississippi who had families, Medgar had trained his family how to respond in the event of a bombing or shooting. His family had grown accustomed to this terrible fear for many years, so when it happened no doubt they hit the floor when the shot rang out. However, although one realizes these tragedies might happen, no one is ever quite prepared to accept this kind of thing. Myrlie Evers peeled the door open to find her husband mortally wounded. Medgar Evers died within the hour.

Whitehead testified that he recalled Beckwith leaving the car with a suitcase-like package but returned without it. He insisted he had gotten out of there in a hurry, and driven the ninety-two miles back to Greenwood in slightly less than one hour. He stated that during most of the way the speedometer registered one hundred twenty miles an hour.

The night Medgar was killed, the mass meeting in Greenwood was over about the same time it was over in Jackson. We officers went over to the Reverend Tucker's house, talking until one o'clock in the next morning. At exactly one o'clock, Tucker received a telephone call. A voice said, "I killed that damned Medgar, and we're going to get you next." Then the caller hung up.

No one thought it was serious, so the Reverend Tucker called Jackson for confirmation. He was told Medgar had been shot and was believed to be dead. We all sat there for the rest of the night. We called some members of the local branch. They came with handguns, rifles and shotguns — anything they could find to protect Reverend Tucker.

The news of Medgar's death traveled like running water. After Beckwith was arrested and jailed in Jackson, it was reported that he was treated more like a guest than a suspect. It was stated also that he had almost all the comforts of a home.

Following the death of Medgar, there was a series of riots, break-ins, and looting in Greenwood and Jackson. Blacks were very angry. His death, in its perturbing way, had given the movement more power. Many Negroes in Mississippi felt somehow responsible for his death, because of the lack of unity and commitment by some. They felt if all blacks in Mississippi were united, Medgar would not have been such an outstanding target. We understood that whites felt killing Medgar would signal the end of the movement.

Medgar Evers's death did not end the civil rights movement in Mississippi, just as Jesus's death did not end Christianity. Hitler thought by killing six million Jews, he would stop the progress of Jews, but it did not. It only made these people more compulsive to do more and to make sure they were never vulnerable again. As the result of Medgar's death, blacks in Greenwood and in the rest of the country became more determined to overcome.

Eyewitnesses testified that Beckwith was in Jackson the night of Medgar's death. Beckwith's lawyer argued that he could not have committed the murder at a quarter to twelve and driven back to Greenwood by one o'-clock a.m. Beckwith was acquitted twice and given a parade down the main street of Greenwood. He became a big man around Greenwood. And as far as I know he is still a Klansmen.

Ironically, on June 12, 1963, the same night Medgar Evers was murdered, President John F. Kennedy gave his famous civil rights speech. Evers's assailant, Byron De La Beckwith, was a Greenwood fertilizer salesman and member of the Citizens' Council.

A braggart and die-hard racist, he was branded a hero by his comrades while he awaited trial. He wouldn't have been incarcerated at all, if the NAACP hadn't insisted.

Beckwith's defense attorney, Hardy Lott, was past president of the Citizens' Council. The acquittal came in spite of the efforts of the prosecutor, William L. Waller, a white man who had zealously attempted to convict Beckwith. During the trial, Beckwith boldly and ceremoniously awarded Waller a box of cigars for his valiant effort to avenge the death of a "nigger" named Medgar Evers. As J. W. Milam and Roy Bryant had done during their trial for the murder of Emmett Till, Beckwith treated the whole procedure as a big joke.

Governor Ross Barnett is reported to have said about the murder of Medgar Evers, "Apparently, it was a dastardly act." Beckwith had only pulled the trigger, while white Mississippians had given him permission. The governor's comment was outrageously hypocritical, and spoke volumes about the ugliness and shamelessness of the institution of racism that extended from the top down.

If Beckwith hadn't carried out the plan to assassinate Medgar Evers, some other white racist would probably have done so. Medgar was very much hated by white Mississippians who were determined not to yield to integrationists. Years passed before Byron De La Beckwith was convicted for the murder of Medgar Evers.

Daddy and Mama attended Medgar Evers's funeral in Jackson. Mama said there was tremendous grief, as well as anger, among the three thousand or more mourners, a crowd that included Martin Luther King, Jr.

"Andrew really loved Medgar Evers," said Mama, describing the effect of the assassination on Daddy. "He thought the world of him. And he was always repeating what Medgar had said or what Medgar had done after one of the mass meetings in Greenwood. Medgar was just four or five years older, but Andrew idolized him. He was a great role model for your father." Medgar Evers, of course, was a great role model for all people.

I also remember the assassination of John F. Kennedy. Mama was combing my hair while the event was being rebroadcast on our black-and-white console TV set. She was sitting on the bed, and I was sitting between her legs on the floor. I was in the second grade, and she was getting me ready for school. I remember Mama's tears wetting my hair. She was overwhelmed with emotion. I was very tender-headed, but I didn't open my mouth when she gathered up my thick hair and brought the comb through the knots.

In my own way, I guess, I realized my little suffering was nothing compared to that of the terror-stricken white woman whose husband's body had fallen over, a bullet in his head. From all indications, especially my mother's reaction, I could see that this had been a good white man, and that the pretty woman was probably nice as well. I felt sad as I walked to school with my sisters Bernice and Mary.

It was November 22, 1963, a date I shall always remember. Its significance was like the birth and crucifixion of Christ. It was a day of uniqueness because of a terrible happening that clouded the sky, overshadowing an insidious hate that permanently snuffed out the life of this man. His death left a hole in the presidency to be replenished once more by a new president, signifying that life must go on. Notwithstanding that, many unanswered questions and untied ends still hung loose in the minds of blacks all over this country. It became clear in the minds and hearts of blacks that anyone who stood for fair play and justice in this country for Negroes would be killed. This has gone on ever since the birth of this country.

I had no comprehension of politics, but I was disturbed about this man's death because my parents were affected emotionally. My thoughts were those of a child, and I had no real concept of what was going on in our country between black people and white people.

After the assassinations of Medgar Evers and John Kennedy, the civil rights struggle in Greenwood forged ahead. Many leaders emerged, and my father was one of them.

"Who else is going to see to it that the blacks in this country are able to achieve what is rightfully ours, if we the blacks do not demand it for ourselves?" I challenged.

Blackballed in Mississippi

Blackballed in Mississippi

After the death of Medgar Evers, many blacks in Greenwood were more determined than ever to register to vote. Throughout Mississippi and the South, the white power structure could no longer completely suppress black activism. Change was gradual, and there was still white resistance. The Citizens' Council, being the most organized effort, was backed by the KKK. If it had not been for the interest of the northern media in the civil rights struggle, the organizing of blacks would have taken longer, and more blacks would have been lynched.

"Who speaks for black people?" Was the question of blacks in Mississippi following the ambush of Medgar Evers. After the uprising, an epidemic of despair descended upon the blacks of the Magnolia State. Yet a determination to escalate the movement for civil rights outweighed downhearted feelings. There was to be no turning back.

That year a national convention of the NAACP was held in Chicago. I was sent there from our branch as a delegate. I met many interesting people, black and white. They were disturbed and intrigued by my name tag, which displayed my name and the state I was from: Andrew L. Jordan, Greenwood, Mississippi. I almost felt like I was the guest of honor. Everyone wanted to buy me something, from a martini to a porterhouse steak.

They seemed to have particular interests in Mississippi. I was asked if I was afraid to go back. I replied that everyone who worked in the civil rights movement in Mississippi was afraid, but that we had no other choice but to stand up for our rights.

I spent two days at the convention. On the morning of the second day I noticed that at the front entrance of the Morrison Hotel stood statues of two black jockeys. I observed them momentarily as all kinds of things ran through my mind. I felt, "Here we are at the national convention and these two statues representing servitude would only disenfranchise the very meaning and concept of the NAACP." Dismayed by this, I talked to some of the other delegates about it. The next day the statues were covered with large cardboard boxes. The young people were not satisfied with that. They argued that the statues should be taken up or the convention be moved. I don't know what became of that.

I returned home with a renewed determination to fight for the cause of justice, no matter the price. Also while I was in Chicago, a march in the honor of Medgar was executed in the streets and led by Mayor Daley and other civil rights leaders.

Back in Mississippi, Charles Evers, Medgar's brother, picked up the baton. Charles was different from Medgar, but led like him in many ways. He was more forcible. His tone of voice also sounded more militant, whereas Medgar's voice, although firm, had been much softer. Medgar had done well in the nine years he carried the ball. The timing was good for Charles, and the stage had been set for the escalation of the movement. We accepted his leadership and followed him to achieve many victories. There weren't many victories in Greenwood, but in other parts of the state where blacks were nearly 100 percent in population, a lot of yardage was made.

As Daddy's involvement increased, so did the risks. Formerly, when others had attempted to register, Daddy was always encouraged to wait until more progress had been made. But people were still losing jobs left and right, and bricks or Molotov cocktails were being thrown into their homes. Daddy lost his teaching position.

When Daddy went to the county courthouse to register to vote, Mama, his partner, went along to do the same. "Andrew and I had talked about it the night before," Mama said, remembering the circumstances of that eventful day. "We talked about what could happen to us and what happened to other black people who attempted to register. But we felt that this was something we had to do. It didn't seem right to Andrew that he could solicit memberships and encourage others to register to vote, but not attempt to register himself. So in support of his decision, I went down with him. We had talked it through, but we were not fully prepared for the repercussions of that decision."

When Daddy and Mama went to register, they were part of COFO (Council of Federated Organizations), the combined effort of SNCC, the NAACP, and CORE to get blacks registered. Fifty to a hundred would-be black voters attempted to register a couple of times a week in a concerted effort to break down the resistance. In 1963, Daddy was the only schoolteacher in Greenwood to attempt to register, and he was fired. Mama tells the story: "Andrew and I went down that day by ourselves. He felt if we went without a group, we would have a better chance of getting registered. We were all dressed up. Andrew had on a brown suit, and I had on a nice blue dress. We looked very professional. We looked prestigious and we felt that way, too."

Mama said that Martha Lamb, the deputy registrar, was the nastiest and rudest woman she had ever met. "That woman hated black people. She had a reputation all over Greenwood for how she treated blacks. We were treated no differently. When Andrew and I got up to the window, she shoved two forms into our faces. Andrew didn't say a word. He just picked up the forms and led me over to the counter along the wall. Personally, I was not even affected by her attitude. We had reached the point where we just saw racist whites as just ignorant and beneath us."

The form was a questionnaire about the Mississippi state constitution. Sometimes this test was administered orally to would-be registrants. My parents had to interpret the state constitution to Martha Lamb's satisfaction. Of course, they didn't have a chance, although they had taken citizenship classes and had gone over the document thoroughly. They probably knew it better than she did. When Mama and Daddy finished the test that was for black registrants only, they walked back up to the counter. Illiterate white citizens of Mississippi could vote without any restrictions.

Mama continued, "When we finished the test that had our names and occupations on it, she snatched it out of our hands. Andrew and I watched as she looked it over. Then she looked at your father with pure hatred and picked up the phone. Andrew and I looked at each other in disbelief. We didn't know what to expect. Then we knew, when she said, 'Give me the superintendent of Tchula schools.' That is where Andrew was teaching at the time. 'I have a nigger named Andrew Jordan over here in Greenwood trying to register to vote,' Martha Lamb told them. Andrew and I went home. We knew our lives were going to change."

In Mississippi we were bound to achieve the goals of what Medgar had tried to do. The fight went on. More blacks across the country were beaten and killed. Many were harassed by policemen, and many were fired from their jobs when they tried to vote or because they were members of the NAACP, SNCC or CORE (Congress of Racial Equality). As my involvement grew in the movement, I was dismissed from a teaching job that I held in Tchula, Mississippi. I was not able to get another teaching position in the state of Mississippi from that period on.

The only income Daddy had after losing his teaching job was from his position as secretary of the Greenwood chapter of the NAACP. After numerous and vain attempts to find another teaching assignment, he worked the job full-time. But he had made a mistake; when asked by the headquarters how much he could live on, he told them thirty-five dollars a week. With seven mouths to feed, rent, and utilities, this was impossible. Within a short time Daddy and Mama were having a difficult time making ends meet.

"Many times the refrigerator would be empty and we would have just beans or rice and cornbread to eat," said Mama, describing that time. "Our lights and gas would be turned off. We couldn't pay our bills, so bill collectors were constantly at the door. Some white man even threatened us over the phone. He said things like, 'Andrew is lucky he ain't dead for being involved with all that mess.' It was scary. It was the worse time of our lives."

Mama said Daddy went all over town trying to make extra money, but no one would hire him. "We couldn't get any credit. Everybody in town knew what had happened. It was very humiliating."

When a mean-talking white man showed up with the sheriff and took every stick of furniture in the house, including the television set Mama and Daddy owed only fifteen dollars on, we found ourselves in a dire predicament. An eviction notice that soon followed was the breaking point. "We ended up being just like the other poor blacks who were receiving government handouts and shipments of food from the North. We lost everything," Mama recalls.

Daddy, being very proud, was ashamed when he couldn't provide for his family. Our only income was the inadequate stipend he was receiving from the NAACP. Accepting handouts from other family members was the only way we could survive. Money and food came primarily from Mama's parents, because they were the only ones who could afford to spare a few dollars.

Granddaddy's weekly visits from the country were a big relief for Mama, who had to scrape together meals for us. He brought us candy and other treats. When the situation became unbearable, my parents sent us to stay out in the country. When all was lost, Mama and Daddy joined us. The Greenwood civil rights movement continued without Daddy.

For Daddy and others like him, the early 1960s was a terrifying time in our history. It was an especially turbulent time for black Mississippians directly involved in the civil rights movement. But, as the movement progressed, blacks were not the only ones in danger of beatings and lynchings; whites were, too, as college students joined in, especially through CORE and SNCC during Freedom Summer in 1964. Because of the Summer Project, northern presses were heavily monitoring Mississippi.

The boycotting of white businesses had a great impact on the struggle. Rather than go out of business, white owners were forced to alter their practices. Voting and school desegregation remained the most difficult issues around the state, and Greenwood was no exception.

When I started first grade in 1962, there were no white children at McLawn Elementary School. My sister Bernice had started school two years before, and she had no white kids in her classroom either. I asked her because I was curious about white kids. I wanted to know what their skin and hair looked like close up. I had seen pictures in magazines, but I knew pictures could be altered. The absurd-looking caricature cartoons of black men, with enormous lips and eyes popping out of wide sockets, didn't look like any colored people I knew. At any rate, it was almost fifteen years after the Supreme Court's 1954 decision ending segregated schools before Greenwood High School allowed black kids to sit next to white kids.

Voting rights for blacks came long before schools desegregated, and long after "white only" signs came down in public places throughout Mississippi. As a result of the 1964 Civil Rights Act and the 1964 Public Accommodations Act, city parks, libraries, movie theaters, some restaurants, and other establishments gradually took down the signs, allowing blacks to mingle with whites instead of being segregated.

But nervous black patrons, remembering the college student and teacher activists, blacks and whites, who had been beaten and had had ketchup, mustard, and sugar dumped over their heads at the Woolworth's lunch counter in Jackson, were very skeptical about eating in certain public places. It was obvious from the blatant stares of whites that they were not wanted, and such situations were potentially violent. Also, they had to wait a long time to be served, because whites were always served first.

Many blacks in Greenwood preferred to continue to hang out on Johnson Street. The right to vote was one thing; eating alongside resentful whites was another. Those who could afford it had to wonder whether eating a nice juicy steak was worth possibly receiving burnt food or meals that might have spit or something worse seasoning them. Yet the blacks who braved these establishments were enforcing the law, and their actions led to eventual improvements in the situation.

Another form of discrimination used at the time was membership qualification; that is, one could not patronize a certain establishment without becoming a member. The number-one prerequisite was white skin. In Greenwood, the Krystal Klub and the Traveler's Inn became membership-only establishments. Other places throughout the South, as well as in the North, followed. At considerable cost, privileged upper-class whites absolutely refused to integrate with blacks. When the city park in Greenwood integrated, whites who could afford it joined the local country club. The park, always immaculately kept when it was for whites only, was soon neglected by the city.

I remember once our family was driving past a white-only park in a small town in Mississippi. We girls were sitting in the back seat behind Mama and Daddy. Since Bernice and I were the oldest, we had the window seats and the better view. On my side I could see a park where the grass was a lush, deep green. Neatly trimmed hedges bordered a chain-link fence that enclosed the park. The hedges made it difficult to see inside, but I could make out the tops of little white boys' and girls' heads, as they sailed up to the bluest sky. They appeared to be having the best fun in the world. I nudged my sisters and soon all of us were looking out the back window, whining for my parents to stop.

Daddy drove right on past. When we got back into Green-wood, he took us to McLawn Elementary School, where we hap-pily scampered out of the back seat of his black-and-white Buick. At this point we girls didn't care. We were overjoyed to have an opportunity to play. Evone, the baby, with her little puffy hands, wiped the tears from her two-year-old face. She put her too-short legs out onto the ground and hurried to catch up with us.

Of course, there was a big difference between that colored-school playground of asphalt and rickety swings and the park where those white children were enjoying a privileged life. But, as young children at the time, we didn't care. We had a mother and a father, two sets of grandparents, a host of other interest-ing relatives, and plenty of Popsicles.

Later that same summer, my parents bought us our very own swing set. This was their way of making us feel privileged. By not pointing out to us the discrepancies, they tried to make cer-tain we didn't feel bad about being discriminated against. They probably hoped we older children wouldn't notice. Naturally, as we grew older, Bernice and I couldn't help but notice and won-der about it.

Although tall hedges surrounded white playgrounds, we were not deterred from peering through the gaps. The "white only" signs on the chain-link fences around these places made them even more intriguing. There seemed to be acres of grass that children could run through and big trees around which they could play tag and hide-and-seek. These playgrounds had loads of equipment: dozens of swings, a couple of sliding boards, several seesaws, a sand box, and monkey bars where children could climb or sit and play house. Park benches provided places for people to sit and read or lie down. Bernice and I could only imagine what else the play areas had that made them better than our own.

On the rare occasions when my sisters and I went swimming, we were just happy to be around other kids. We didn't have many opportunities to play with other black children because we were in the country most of the time. So, while the recreational facilities were definitely inferior for black children, we were still able to enjoy what was for us a novel experience.

Before the park opened to blacks, Mama and Daddy had taken us for picnics in the country, and, though we enjoyed these precious family moments, there were no swings or sliding boards out in the woods. So we were glad when the park took down the "white only" sign. But when white parents saw black children like us in the park, they stopped bringing their kids. Mama said the city stopped mowing the grass and trimming the hedges and just let the place go.

Of course, Greenwood was not unique in its resistance to integration. These kinds of situations happened all over the country. As places were integrated, more private clubs were established, and public facilities became neglected. Blacks who could afford the membership fees at private establishments were excluded by further rules. For instance, to become a member one might have to be invited by another member, or to be an alumnus of a particular school, or to have so many references. As blacks continued to challenge the status quo, whites came up with new obstacles.

As the efforts to integrate continued, so did the violence. In June of 1964, segregationists led by Klan/police officers beat and murdered two whites, Mickey Schwerner and Andrew Goodman, and a black student named James Chaney. The search for their bodies brought in the FBI and hundreds of news reporters from across the country. The bodies of the three innocent young men were found in a landfill in Philadelphia, Mississippi.

More students might have died if federal agents had not swarmed across the state. Many locals were peeved, believing that it had taken the killing of whites to create outrage in the rest of the country, especially in the White House. However, over time, they became more grateful and less resentful. The students, black and white, coming from schools such as Harvard, Yale, and Howard, possessed much-needed skills, and they helped push the agenda of the civil rights movement to the forefront of American politics. Blacks and whites living and working together in the heart of the South was a force to be reckoned with. The benefits from a united force would not and could not be denied.

My father was pleased that the movement had gained national attention, and he welcomed the outsiders. He believed that Mississippi needed all people, black and white, working together to turn the vicious tide of racism.

So, early in 1964, while these students were coming into Mississippi and working in freedom schools to help improve the deficient academic skills of impoverished black children, helping blacks register to vote, and organizing and engaging in sit-ins, Daddy was making plans to move his family north.

He and Mama had talked it over with their parents, and they all agreed it was the only solution. Daddy called his brother Clevester in Toledo, and found that he would be happy to let us stay with him and his wife in their big childless house until we got on our feet.

The truth of the matter is that Daddy had again come to the realization that he had Mama and five girls to provide for. Once again he was forced to put his family's well-being first. And once again he felt like a coward who was deserting the movement. Although Daddy had lost his career and his possessions, he still felt he needed to do more. The decision to leave Mississippi was not an easy one; it was forced on him. He had lost his job, and no one would hire him because of his involvement in the civil rights movement. He had no other options. He had to make a living.

My father deeply loved Mississippi because it was his home, and all of us had been born there. We all loved Mississippi and lamented leaving it.*

---

*After finishing this book, I learned that there had been some controversy surrounding my father regarding NAACP financial matters at the time he left Mississippi. My response to this thirty-seven-year-old rumor is to say that, according to my mother, in the following years when we visited the state my father always stopped by the Greenwood NAACP office and was always well received: no one confronted him with any allegations, and he never referred to any problems. When my uncle, David Jordan, started the Greenwood Voter's League in 1965, no such issues were raised. In 1988, my father spoke at a rally and was greeted with admiration and respect.

I was in the eighth grade and I could read well. I had a great love for books, and I read everything I could find except comic books. But I was always puzzled by much of the literature I read. Everything I read was written about white people and by white people. I wondered why.

I thought the irises of all white people's eyes were sky blue. Where I got this notion, I don't know. Daddy didn't tell me. (He rarely talked about white folks at home, although he was involved in the struggle and white people were the cause of our dilemma.) It was certainly not from anyone in school, where I only saw names scratched out at the front of first-grade readers, because, as when Daddy was a child, my class got the raggedy, hand-me-down books. Perhaps in those books the characters Sally, Dick, and Jane had blue eyes; I haven't seen one of the readers since my days at McLawn Elementary, and I can't recall.

"See Sally run. Run, Dick, run. Run, run, run." This is what I learned to read in school. Thankfully, since my father was a teacher, he was able to supplement my education with more stimulating books.

I didn't know anything about the white kids who lived on the other side of town. I had never seen a white boy or girl up close, at least not that I could recall. I wondered if their voices were gay and musical like my sister's and mine, as we laughed and stumbled over too many words falling from our lips in our excitement to tell a story. And did white children have voices full of mirth like ours because summer was a big juicy watermelon full of endless seeds? How we loved to eat ice-cold watermelon on the back steps of Grandmama's porch. Did white kids have seed-spitting contests, as we did? I had no idea what white kids were like; they were a mystery to me. I didn't know what the word "stereotype" meant. I looked forward to summer and watermelon. My sisters did, too.

The first time I saw a white boy up close enough to tell if white people really had blue eyes was in 1964, the summer after Mama and Daddy and my two younger sisters drove up Highway 49E in our loaded-down Buick. They looked like displaced nomads, with plastic-covered boxes of clothes tied up in several bundles on top of the car. They were in for a long journey to Toledo, where Uncle Clevester was. The back seat was packed so high with clothes that Evone and Velma had to sit up front between Mama and Daddy. An eight-bottle carton of Coca-Cola and a basket of fried chicken were placed between Mama's slender legs on the floor. Daddy had always jokingly declared, "Arella's legs are so skinny that you can put them in a match box."

I was jealous of my younger sisters and too old to be wishing I was the baby. We girls knew Daddy was being run out of town, and he looked worried and sad. He wasn't walking very tall when he placed the last box in a little space he found in the trunk. Nor was Daddy yanking on one of my long plaits as he often did when he was being affectionate. He looked like a man wandering aimlessly out of Mississippi, not sure how his life was going to turn out.

I don't remember having any eye contact with my father during the period when part of our family was making ready to leave Mississippi. Daddy and I had always seemed to be able to communicate by telepathy, but it wasn't happening during that period. He was in a world of his own, and I, who was just crazy about Daddy, was not privy to it. I sensed that he must have felt a loss of dignity now that white folks had stripped him of his teaching profession. Mama didn't look too chipper either. She had been crying all that week. So Daddy certainly didn't need to see fat tears dropping from my big eyes. He needed my support, and I needed to be strong. It was going to be hard for me to survive four months without either of my parents.

Bernice, Mary, and I were to stay with our grandparents out in the country until Mama and Daddy came back to get us. They left in May and were supposed to return for us in September. Mr. Jeff was still planting cotton around my grandparents' house, so the green plants were thriving when they left. By the time Mama and Daddy were due to return, cotton balls were sure to be all over the place.

That summer felt like ten years. I got into a good bit of mischief, and a huge lump was always in my throat because I missed Daddy and Mama a lot. It felt as though they had gone off to some strange land far away. And since we didn't have a phone in the country, we couldn't talk to our parents that whole time.

I got to see a white boy up close because I got stung by wasps. Bernice was really to blame because she was hitting at the mud nest that was minding its own business in the corner of Miss Elizabeth's vine-and-flower-covered porch. Miss Elizabeth lived less than a quarter-mile up the dirt road from my grandparents. She was keeping us because they had gone into Greenwood to do some shopping; my other sister, Mary, had gone with them.

I was sitting on the rotting top step of her house. My flip-flop-clad feet were resting on the second step. My head, with its

161

three plaits — one on top and two on the sides — rested solemnly in my hands. Occasionally, I would look over my shoulder at Bernice, who was ten years old, tall, slightly bowlegged, and beanpole skinny in her green shorts set and yellow flip-flops. She was balancing herself on the creaking, unpainted, uneven, sloping porch floor, which was gray like the rest of the crooked, leaning house. All the ones on the plantation, including my grandparents', were gray — not painted, just washed-out, weather-beaten gray.

Bernice was messing with those wasps, going out of her way to aggravate them. She had even gone around the porch swing to pester them by waving Miss Elizabeth's broom over their nest. They were minding their own business, doing whatever wasps do. I was merely waiting to see what was going to happen. Perhaps I was enjoying an idyllic, lazy summer day or was fighting back tears because I felt abandoned., I certainly didn't deserve what happened to me.

Those wasps simply got sick and tired of Bernice antagonizing them. About two dozen of them swarmed out of their military base, like black Tuskegee airmen in search of German planes. Bernice was their menace, not I. But I had no time to declare my innocence or defend myself when they made their first attack to the left side of my head. Bernice, being in a better position, ran safely into Miss Elizabeth's house, which smelled of chewing tobacco. Miss Elizabeth, who had been dozing in her rag-bound rocking chair, jumped up, startled, when she heard the screen door slam. In her alarm, she nearly knocked over her spit jar.

"What's wrong with y'all chillins?" she sputtered as best she could through the plug of tobacco in her jaw. (How she could sleep and keep from swallowing her spittle was a mystery to us kids. Sometimes the brown saliva would ooze down the side of her mouth when she slept.) I heard Bernice through the screen door answering breathlessly something about bees coming out. I don't know how she explained it to Miss Elizabeth or whether she admitted that she was the cause of the war. Bernice was probably amazed by the turn of events. I was out there fighting for my life, being stung repeatedly about the head, while she was safe in the house. Miss Elizabeth reached down by the door and retrieved her weapon — a mosquito-spraying can, which in those days was the kind of insect-killing device that required one to use both hands. One hand held it steady, while the other pulled and pushed the pump. At the end of the pump was a refillable round container that held the mosquito repellent. The entire contraption was made of metal. The only problem was that I was being attacked by wasps, not mosquitoes. What's more, Miss Elizabeth took too long to get outside. She was too old, too slow, and too late.

Screaming like a fool, I dashed around the house and all over Miss Elizabeth's marigolds. I ran through the cotton field and scratched my legs and thighs up to my red cut-off shorts. My arms got scratched up, too, since the red-and-white shirt I was wearing didn't offer much protection. I ran out of my new red flip-flops, leaving one in a cotton row and one alongside the road. I raced all the way to my grandparents' house. Still screaming, I banged on the door, having forgotten that they weren't back from town. The wasps had turned back before I hit the cotton field.

When, after a few days I looked worse instead of better, Grandmama felt she needed to take me into Greenwood to see the doctor. We walked up to the highway, which was about two miles up the road. Back then the Greyhound, coming from Memphis, would stop alongside a store on Highway 49. The store had long been closed, but the bus would stop if someone was standing out where the driver could see him or her. The driver ran a scheduled route, and Negroes on the Cole plantation would pay a fare and ride on into Greenwood.

When the bus stopped, Grandmama and I got on. Right away the driver remarked on my appearance. Grandmama told him what had occurred and said that she was taking me to the doctor. The bus driver said I must be allergic to wasps to swell up so bad.

Grandmama said, "Yes, sir, I reckon she may well be."

I remember thinking he was a nice white man to be so concerned about me. We sat down near the middle of the half-full bus. When we took our seats, I saw the white boy. He was about my age or maybe a year younger. The boy was looking back at me, and I was leaning out of my seat to look up the aisle at him. We looked and looked at each other. When I think about him today I have to chuckle. He must have thought I was strange looking or perhaps deformed, and I thought he was quite interesting looking as well.

On that day, I wondered if the boy's life was anything like mine. I wondered if he had a mother who could cook the best black-eyed peas and corn bread. Did he have a schoolteacher daddy who corrected his grammar every time he opened his mouth? Did he have all boys in his family, or sisters, or one of each? I wondered if wasps had ever attacked him. I somehow doubted it, though he might have been bitten by mosquitoes. I wondered if he had ever played with Negro children. Was he as nice as Dick and Jane? He seemed to be. He probably also had a dog named Spot. At that point in my life, that is all I knew about white kids.

I was very curious about this white boy who sat half-turned in his seat, with one dingy, broken-stringed tennis shoe placed solidly on the black rubber mat that ran the length of the bus. One of his lightly freckled bare arms was placed on the back of the seat in front of him and the other on the seat just to the right of his blue-jean-clad thigh. He was turned so that he could get a good look at me and also keep himself balanced as he bounced slightly in the seat.

Yes, the boy's eyes were indeed blue. They were not a clear sky blue but a grayish steel blue. His crew-cut hair was more a tannish color than yellow blond. He had a snubbed nose and very small lips. His features were different from those of any Negro children whom I knew. I had to look at him a long time, because my eyes were nearly closed from the wasp stings and my vision wasn't so good. I couldn't see the woman he was sitting with, except for the back of her snow-white hair. I figured he was also traveling with his grandmother. He didn't say anything, so I never heard his voice. While I studied that kid, I forgot about my own appearance.

I didn't stop looking at him until Grandmama pulled on the back of my polka-dotted, pink-and-white sundress, forcing me to sit back in my seat. Twice when the bus had jostled, I had nearly fallen out of my seat, because I was leaning out so far in my attempt to see the boy. Later that evening when Grandmama gave me my medicine, she teased me about looking so hard at the boy that I forgot to be self-conscious about my appearance. But, judging from the way he stared back, he was curious about me as well. He probably wondered what had gotten hold of that colored girl.

Even before that summer when we stayed with my grandparents, Bernice and I had spent a great deal of time in the country, visiting and helping Grandmama and Granddaddy in their store. When we were there, it was our job to dust, stock the shelves, and keep the candy case sparkling clean. Granddaddy taught us how to count money so we could wait on the colored kids who trickled in from the cotton fields with fifty cents or a quarter. Sometimes on the Fridays and Saturdays after payday, they'd have a dollar or two. On those days they would buy lots of items. Bernice was rather shy, so I waited on the kids most of the time.

To this day, my granddaddy mocks me by curling his lips and saying in a proper-sounding voice, "Boooys, can I help y'all?" Apparently I thought of myself as mighty important when I was playing proprietor. It was fun for Bernice and me at our grandparents', and we always had plenty to eat.

My sister Mary Ella was just like me when she waited on the country kids, except that she would eat junk the whole time and not just when Granddaddy told us to get something for ourselves. Eventually, when Granddaddy discovered Mary was on her third candy bar and was eating up the profits, he gave her the job of toting water from the well. Although she was only about six years old, Mary was very strong. She could do that chore in no time. She would half-run, half-walk, splashing water all over her legs, until she had the six tin buckets placed on the back porch for our baths later in the evening. Before Granddaddy could say, "Maayella, go tote the water," Mary would be back in the store flirting with the colored boys, another thing she liked to do, in addition to eating up the goodies.

Grandmama had opened the store in 1958, the year Velma was born. Actually, Granddaddy provided the funds, which he had saved up from selling whiskey. But we always called it Grand-mama's store because she really ran the place. She had been in business for nearly six years that summer.

"Velma? Little Bit? It's Henry Wright."

Colored folks would call her name through the latched screen door at the front of the house, where the combination kitchen-store was located. Grandmama, having seen them walk or drive up, usually knew who the visitors were before they could an-nounce themselves. She would say, "Here comes Henry Wright" or whatever the name was. When they got to just about the middle of the yard, Grandmama would rise out of her chair by the window, where she had been watching nothing in particular. She would then tidy her hair and smooth her clothes down.

On those occasions when she didn't feel like waiting on a too-talkative customer, she would have me wait on him or her. She would slightly close the door to the bedroom where she was sit-ting, and listen to the transaction. If the bill was too large or the customer needed a pound of bologna or cheese, she would come to the rescue before I even had to call her.

If it was someone Grandmama didn't recognize, she would ask plenty of questions through the screen door, until the person eventually said he was related to so-and-so, or said something that made her comfortable. If, after this scrutiny, she still didn't feel at ease, she would tell the person to come back when her husband was home. The screen door would stay latched until someone else came along or Granddaddy arrived. Granddaddy was seldom gone more for than an hour during the day, so the customer wouldn't have to sit under the pecan tree for too long. In any case, Grandmama would have her pistol in her hand, ready for any funny business.

Grandmama also made out the list of goods that had to be bought from the warehouse in Greenwood. Some delivery people would come rumbling down the dirt road to make stops, the Wonder Bread and Coca-Cola trucks being two that I remember. Grandmama kept her shelves lined with rows of all kinds of canned goods, as well as bags of flour, sugar, rice, cornmeal, and noodles. She also sold Mail Pouch chewing tobacco, Pall Mall, Camel, and Kool cigarettes, and Prince Albert cigars.

On top of the candy case was a glass jar of peppermint sticks. Cookies were in separate containers: oatmeal, macaroon, and sugar. A big paraffin-covered round of Colby cheese sat on a small table next to the oatmeal cookies. Oatmeal cookies and cheese sandwiches were my favorites. In a freezer alongside the wall, Grandmama kept boxes of sausages, neckbones, beef, and whole chickens that she sold to the sharecroppers and field hands who had iceboxes or were going to cook them that evening for supper. Lunch meats such as bologna and salami were kept cold in the icebox along with the milk and soda pop.

On special occasions like the Fourth of July, she would sell whole plates of hot cooked meals like barbecued ribs, pork sandwiches, chicken, and sausages. Alongside the meat she would have potato salad, greens, and macaroni and cheese. Granddaddy would barbecue in a huge steel drum placed horizontally on stilts, right behind the empty clothesline. He would laugh, joke around, and work with the meat all day long. His buddies,

Henry Wright, Sugarman, Mr. Plute, Ol' Bro Fate, and others would stay all day, sitting on upturned bottle crates and playing checkers with bottle tops under the spread of an enormous pecan tree.

If it was hog-killing time, Granddaddy would slap sandwiches together until nearly midnight. These times were just grand, because happy, grinning black folks would come and go all day long. Naturally, we girls had to stay out the way, and, of course, we could not get into any grown folks' conversations. Grandmama was worse than Mama about this. Our duties were to fetch RC Colas or other items for folks who asked for something to drink or eat.

Most important, we had to remember to ask for reimbursement when we handed over the goods. Grandmama was certain to whisper, "Did Mrs. Lloyd pay you fifteen cents for that orange drink?" We called it Grandmama's store because she saw to the business side of running it. But if she couldn't get folks to pay up their credit, then Granddaddy, after closing the store in the evening, would take the books and collect door to door. Rarely did he have a problem getting his money.

We never had any misgivings visiting my grandparents' house. We loved staying out in the country, and we felt safe there. Granddaddy had a gun in the top drawer of a mahogany dresser that was in the hallway leading to the second bedroom. The gun was always loaded, and a box of bullets lay beside it. We were instructed never to touch it. When my grandparents weren't home we would open the drawer to view its black barrel and brown handle, but we never touched it.

While we had many wonderful experiences in the country, we were really city kids, afraid even of the chickens Grandmama raised. So we didn't do much exploring of nature; we were more likely to play indoors with our baby dolls. There were just too many unsavory creatures to contend with in the country — snakes, lizards, and bugs. We didn't relish unpleasant surprises like lizards slithering over bare feet. There were, however, some wonderful creatures that we liked to observe, such as butterflies, grasshoppers, daddy longlegs, and yellow baby chicks.

Summertime at my grandparents' house meant beautiful days and nights, and it was so quiet that we could hear the sounds of whooping birds, chirping crickets, croaking frogs, and a dog barking way up the road. In the early morning hours, the hoot of an owl could be heard in the little clump of trees directly behind the house. We could hear a car coming up the road long before we saw the cloud of dust. Many times we all stood and watched the cloud getting nearer and nearer, until Granddaddy or Grandmama could announce who was coming.

My grandparents' tin-roofed grocery store/house sat picturesquely underneath the expansive branches of a sweet-meat pecan tree. Another pecan tree of lesser quality and two evergreens lined the front of the house along the road that led to Moles Lake. A barbed-wire fence enclosed the property and kept out stray dogs and other animals that could not slither. A brick path went to the leaning outhouse, which stood approximately fifty yards from the main structure. The house/store was raggedy, small, and patched up, but Bernice, Mary, and I thought it was magnificent, better than any grand mansion — except for the outhouse. None of us girls ever got used to it. It's a wonder we weren't always constipated.

In later years, when our family went there to visit, we would travel a route perpendicular to the highway, which was on higher ground. By the second bend in the dirt road, if we were not traveling too fast and the dust could settle a bit, we could see the house. I would always be nervous with anticipation. My sisters were anxious as well. Mama's eyes would sparkle and tear up, and a smile would play at her lips. For the first few years, Daddy seemed uneasy. Later, after he had become reconciled about leaving Mississippi, he would wear a broad smile as he drove the last quarter-mile home.

This was our experience each time we came back from Ohio to visit. Thankfully, my grandparents and their house would be the same. We were the ones who would have changed. We girls would have grown taller, and our family would show more prosperity — a new car, better clothes — and our accents would sound more northern. We were losing remnants of Mississippi, our home. How funny that we were willing to change but wanted everything to stay the same at that ramshackle house-store, so that we could be home again. Over the years, although our grandparents grew older, they never changed in any real sense. Always their faces would break out in huge grins when they realized that we were the ones in the cloud of dust.

That last summer, in 1964, we knew that when our parents came back we would move to a place called Ohio and leave Mississippi for good. We missed our parents, but we were not all that excited about leaving Granddaddy's stories and Grandmama's store. We soaked up as much Mississippi sun as we could absorb. We were seen and not heard, but we heard and saw a lot. We even saw Granddaddy sell a pint of whiskey or two. We also mutilated dozens of beautiful butterflies.

I feel terrible when I recall how Bernice, Mary, and I believed that old lie. Some silly child up the road told us that if we bit the head off a butterfly, we would get a dress the same color. We should have known better, since the girl was barefooted and as raggedy as a buzzard stalking an old sick cow. But we were gullible and spent a whole day spotting and catching the prettiest butterflies we could find. They were beautiful and plentiful that summer, vivid with colors ranging from yellow and blue polka-dot wings to brownish-orange and sunset red. Had the lie been true, we would have had a trunk full of the most beautiful dresses. We laid out the headless diurnal insects along the porch rail so that we could remember what color dresses we had selected. We weren't, however, barbaric enough to bite off the heads with our teeth. We used Popsicle sticks to do our cowardly deed. We might have carried out this carnage all summer long if Grandmama hadn't asked us whether we were losing our minds.

Also, that sweltering summer, my grandparents kept half a dozen hogs that loved to eat gross meals called "slop." We had to contend with these creatures along with the oppressive heat. The piglets were cute and resembled helpless babies. But we didn't care for them much once they got past the toddler stage.

Once our frantically beating hearts threatened to break through our chests when "Big Daddy Hog" got loose and chased us around the house. Our feet flew faster than Wilma Rudolph's when she broke the world record. Again I lost my flip-flops. But this time I earned a silver medal when I took a flying leap for the back porch. I just barely made it behind long-legged Bernice, and slammed the handmade screen door into the snout of eight hundred pounds of pork blubber.

After hearing all the commotion, Grandmama rushed from the front of the house. A little woman, well under five feet tall and weighing less than one hundred pounds, she could be fierce herself when she got hold of a switch. Her hands on her hipless little frame, she threatened, "If y'all don't quit messin' with that hog, I'm gonna lock that screen door and let him getcha."

Now, just the prospect of that back screen door being locked took all the fun out of teasing "Big Daddy Hog." We had to find some other forms of amusement. A nineteen-inch black-and-white GE, whose rabbit ears only brought in three fuzzy channels, certainly wasn't entertaining us. For some reason, Lawrence Welk's show was one my grandparents liked to watch, and they rarely missed it, fuzzy or not. But the sight of Lawrence Welk grinning and waltzing with some beautiful lady amid thousands of bubbles was not very stimulating for us. Teasing "Big Daddy Hog" could get our adrenaline flowing, and would give us something to talk about for a week. Sometimes we were so bored that we just had to liven things up.

Unfortunately, because of our constant lookout for snakes, lizards, chickens, big green pecan worms, a hog bent on revenge, and Grandmama's switch, we were always too wary of the potential "dangers" to fully appreciate the joys of nature, which made the country setting so idyllic in our youthful days.

We really had a lot of fun that summer. One of the funniest things happened to a good-looking colored man. We didn't know him because he wasn't a local, having come for summer work on the Cole plantation. Mary thought he was just the "coolest looking dude" when he came in to order Pall Mall cigarettes, a chocolate Moon Pie, and an RC Cola. She came giggling to get Bernice and me, who were playing with our paper dolls in the back bedroom. We dropped what we were doing and ran to the front of the house behind Mary. The "cool dude" was just stepping out the door. We waited a few minutes, then slipped out behind him while Granddaddy waited on another customer.

The tall stranger, looking like a black version of the Marlboro Man, perched his narrow behind on the front fence near the mailbox. First he smoked a cigarette; then he opened his Moon Pie. We girls were peering at him from the side of the house. Mary was giggling and grinning excitedly from ear to ear. She could hardly contain herself. Bernice was pensive, and, being the older sister, told Mary to be quiet so he wouldn't know we were spying on him. Of course he'd already seen us; he just wasn't ready to acknowledge that he had.

Princely though he was, I was being distracted by the yellow jackets that were buzzing around his drink. Each time he lifted his muscled, shirt-sleeved arm to sip from the bottle, he absently waved one away. I, of course, had good reason to keep an eye on those insects. They were not wasps, but as far as I was concerned, they were kin. The dude, however, didn't seem the least bit concerned as he continuously waved them away from the mouth of the bottle. He had one foot securing his balance, with the help of a tall evergreen tree, and the other one dangled above the grass at the base of the fence. His RC Cola sat on the rail about a foot from his dusty, jean-clad behind, which had been on a tractor since early morning.

We must have looked at him for a good five minutes before he smiled and waved hello to us. That was all it took to send us scurrying in fits of girlish giggles back into the house. Sheltered as we were, the handsome visitor was like a movie star to us; unbeknownst to him, he would be the love interest in our daydreams for years to come.

I must admit that one of us girls should have warned him that those yellow jackets had a nest up in that tree. I guess I should have. Bernice was too shy, and Mary would have had to press both hands over her mouth to keep from giggling, because she was so enthralled by him. He never would have understood what she was saying. When we last saw that young man he was running to his tractor. Granddaddy and a few other men were laughing and joking in the front yard until they saw him hightailing it out of there.

"Hey, what's the matter, son?" Granddaddy yelled after the retreating man.

When Granddaddy caught up to him, he was backing his tractor out of the yard. He managed to say a few words. We couldn't hear the exchange, but we had some idea what the man's hurry was about, because he was holding his mouth. We ran through the house to the screened porch. We didn't go out into the yard, because we could see the scene from where we were. There by the tree on the ground was our hero's half-eaten Moon Pie and the RC Cola spilling out of the bottle. Simultaneously our mouths fell open in astonishment. Bernice broke first with a squeal of laughter. I thought she would hurt herself, as she was holding her side and bumping against the side of the house. Mary and I also got tickled. Soon the three of us were howling as we clung to support each other before falling into a heap. It was one of the most comical sights we had ever seen. Yellow jackets were feasting on a picnic of Moon Pie and RC Cola spilled in the dirt. Up the road our dream man sped away in a cloud of dust. Yes, I should have warned him, because we never laid eyes on our lover boy again that whole summer.

Although I probably enjoyed that last summer more than my sisters did, I especially missed my father. I was not afraid of farm creatures when Daddy was around. No matter how big I was supposed to be, I was never reluctant to skedaddle up Daddy's legs in an effort to get away from scary stuff.

Always immensely proud of my father, I took great pleasure in telling everyone, especially other children, that "my daddy is a schoolteacher." I assume now it was because it elevated my own status. By declaring this fact, especially to the barefooted colored kids in the country who were not afraid of anything except maternal women with switches, I could look down on them just as they looked down on the Jordan girls, who were "sissies."

If I had one of my frequent earaches, I could sit on Daddy's lap on the screened-in back porch or in the back bedroom while he talked to the country menfolk. They talked a lot about the civil rights movement. Negro men living in the country were isolated from the struggle. Before we left the Delta, when Daddy was in the country with us, they enjoyed visiting with him and catching up on what was happening in Greenwood. These men respected and admired my father, who was very articulate and proper in his speech. They looked up to him and often said so, because he was an "educated man." I liked to listen in on their conversations.

When we learned to sing the freedom song "We Shall Overcome," Daddy taught us how to cross our arms with extended hands so that we could lock hands with one another in a straight line. As we sang the lyrics, we would sway back and forth from side to side. We giggled a lot when we tried to synchronize our swaying, though we were somewhat aware of the seriousness of the song. Mary and I sang that song a lot that summer, while we waited for our parents to come back for us.

Once some white men came around asking questions. Mary answered the front door. By the time they had finished telling her how pretty she was, she had managed to tell them that Daddy and Mama were up in Clevester, Ohio. Mary had the information all mixed up. Daddy's oldest brother, Clevester, had once lived in Cleveland, but now he and his second wife lived in Toledo. Mary said that we were going to be staying with them until we got a place of our own. She was on a roll when Grandmama came to the door and told her to hush up. They laughed and said that Mary had told them her father and mother were in Clevester, Ohio. Grandmama said she didn't know "nothin' about that." They left us standing in the door, worried that what had happened to Medgar Evers might possibly happen to Daddy in Ohio.

We later learned that these men were tracking down Daddy primarily because they wanted to repossess our car. When Daddy couldn't find work in Mississippi, he had fallen behind on the payments. By the time he began working at Interlake Steel in Toledo, where Uncle Clevester worked and had helped him get a job, the repo men had found the car parked in front of my uncle's house on Vermont Street.

In late August, Mama and my younger sisters came home on the Greyhound bus. We were to meet them at the old abandoned store that still served as a bus stop. It was about midday, very warm, after school. We had started school with the other colored kids, and that day as soon as we got off the school bus saw my grandparents waiting to lock up the store so we could drive up to the highway.

I was very excited at the thought of seeing Mama but disappointed that Daddy wouldn't be on the bus. He couldn't take off from his new job. Mama was coming back earlier than expected, which was really nice because we had missed her tremendously.

In school, Mary and I had been silly with nervous energy all that day. Bernice was moody, and as usual she was behaving in a superior way. Some tension was revealed in her face, around her thin lips and angular jawline. She probably realized that before long we would all be headed away, leaving our home and our beloved grandparents.

Evone was the first to step off the bus after the driver, who was opening the baggage compartment to remove Mama's luggage. Then came redheaded Velma, clutching a bag of potato chips. Last was Mama, looking wilted from the long ride. She smiled, though, and made a fuss over us. Apparently Grandmama couldn't plait hair very well with her little stubby fingers. I was ecstatic to see Mama. Our family was almost intact again.

There were smiles, singing and laughter among black people in those days in spite of the difficulties. It was nothing to witness a bunch of people working their hands raw and singing to the top of their voices.

Moving to Ohio

Before we could join Daddy in Toledo, a number of things had to be done. He had to find a place for our family to live. Shortly after Mama came for us girls, Daddy moved out of his brother's house into a one-room boardinghouse closer to work. There, he scrimped and saved nearly every penny, working double shifts so that he could rent a three-bedroom house near his brother's on Vermont Street.

Daddy moved into the house and immediately began saving for our bus fare. He was exhausted and working around the clock. Fortunately, he didn't have to buy any furniture, because the old woman who had lived there had left behind discarded items. As the saying goes, "One man's junk is another man's treasure," and three iron beds, an old plaid sofa, a couple of stuffed chairs, and a dinette set were just what we needed. Daddy picked up other necessities dirt cheap at Goodwill.

While Daddy was in Toledo readying our home, Mama was shipping boxes up north by train. In those boxes, which had been left all summer long on my grandparents' porch, were bed linens, pots, pans, and other household goods. By all appearances, everything was going according to plan. The one event that dampened our spirits and devastated Daddy was the death of his mother, just a week after Mama had come down.

Grandmama Jordan had suffered from diabetes for many years, and her health that summer had worsened. She was nearly blind and had become bedridden. By the time Mama went to visit her, Grandmama was near death. She told Mama that her dead brother had visited her the night before. To Negroes in Mississippi, this was a sure sign that death was coming soon. Grandmama Jordan passed away a few days later.

When Daddy drove home with Uncle Clevester, it was obvious that he had lost weight, and he was dejected as well. It was a difficult situation and a dangerous period for him. Several times that summer after our car was repossessed in Toledo, white men had come out to the country, again asking about Daddy. Mama was there to answer their questions those times. She said they were only bill collectors, but they were making threatening remarks. White men asking for the whereabouts of a former civil rights activist was more than a little disconcerting for our family.

Daddy insisted on all of us going to the wake. I remember that day very well. Bernice didn't want to go because she was frightened of dead people. I wanted to see Grandmama Jordan, because I knew it would be the last time. I had loved her big hugs, and, like Mama, I had enjoyed the way she laughed and joked around.

Lying in the casket, she was dressed for church. Her long hair was beautiful and curled around her pleasant sleeping face. She smelled sweet, as she always did. Daddy kissed his mother. His eyes were wet, and he looked exhausted.

Granddaddy Jordan, who was pretty broken up, was sobbing loudly when we stopped by his house. He was sitting on the front porch in the green glider, grieving over the memory of the sixteen-year-old girl he had eloped with years ago. He and Daddy sat and talked for a while. By the next morning, Daddy and Uncle Clevester were on their way back to Ohio. It was too dangerous for Daddy to go to the funeral. They were in Mississippi for less than twenty-four hours. We barely got a glimpse of this uncle we had never seen before.

Colored people and cotton-picking machines were dotting the fields. The store was busy with folks coming in to buy drinks, bologna sandwiches, and whatever else they had a hankering to eat. Daddy had sent the bus tickets by mail a week before, and he was anxiously waiting in our new home for us to join him.

It was difficult to leave Mississippi, even with the nice new school clothes my grandparents had bought for us. We queried our younger sisters, Velma and Evone, over and over about Toledo. What did the people look like? How did they talk? Are there big buildings in the city? Did you see any colored kids? Did you see any white kids? Even after they tried to tell us, we still couldn't form a picture in our heads, because our younger sisters' recounted experiences were too fragmented and lacked any significant details. They were really too young to express in concrete terms what Ohio was going to be like. And Mama was too busy with the preparations for our leaving to brief us.

Somehow, though, we knew deep down that our lives would change forever. We knew that, in a few days, we wouldn't wake up to the rich green fragrance of the Delta, and the cotton fields that were so much a part of our everyday lives would no longer surround us. To us there could be no other place in the world like Mississippi.

The last cotton we saw was in miles and miles of acreage along the stretch from Money to Memphis. Colored people looked up from their cotton sacks as the Greyhound droned by. They seemed to be saying, "Farewell, Jordan family, we wish you well." I looked at one heavyset woman with a red handkerchief wrapped around her head until she was left behind like the telephone poles whizzing past my window.

She did something that Grandmama hadn't been able to do. Of course, we were not known to that woman who waved her hand in farewell and watched us ride out of sight. She was probably waving in remembrance of a relative who had left her behind years before. That morning, as we left before daybreak, Grandmama couldn't bring herself to say goodbye. Before we boarded the bus, she gave each of us a tearful hug and a soft kiss on the cheek; then she turned her back, unable to watch us leave. Granddaddy's crinkled eyes smiled weakly as he waved us off. It was one of the saddest days I can remember. We were thrilled to be going to live with Daddy, but it was heartbreaking to leave our grandparents and Mississippi.

It was October of 1964 when my mother, my four sisters, and I rode into the Greyhound bus station in Toledo. In Mama's purse was a letter from Daddy and the address of our new home. Daddy had to work, so we were to take a cab. He promised to be home early that evening. It seemed so long since I had seen a genuine smile on his face. I surely missed the "old" Daddy.

Toledo was enormous compared to Greenwood, but seemed smaller than downtown Memphis had appeared to be when we changed buses. We were mesmerized by the sights — people strolling in and out of what we thought were skyscraper buildings and lots of late-model cars going up and down the streets.

We saw mostly white people, very few blacks; Memphis and downtown Toledo were nothing like Greenwood's Johnson Street. Immediately we felt a change coming over us. Now we were living up north. It was a culture shock to say the least.

We got ourselves and our beat-up suitcases into a Yellow Cab and were taken to our new home. Mama sat up front with the talkative driver, and we girls sat rather comfortably in the roomy backseat. We were quiet, being tired from the long eighteen-hour bus ride and still nervous about our new surroundings. When the driver pulled up to the curb of the tree-lined street, he and Mama got out of the vehicle almost simultaneously. My sisters and I leaned around one another, attempting to guess which house was ours. None of us was brave enough to ask Mama. We knew she was exhausted and her nerves probably frayed from having to keep track of us.

Patiently, we waited on the sidewalk as the driver took our belongings from the trunk and walked them one by one to a narrow concrete path leading to a white one-story house with a screened porch. Apparently this was going to be our new home. Mama, seemingly for the hundredth time, was reading over the letter from Daddy. Finally dropping her arm and the wrinkled letter to her side, she said to the driver, "My husband said he'd leave a key on the back porch." The man smiled and nodded his head, indicating that he was willing to wait and that he would take the heavy overstuffed luggage into the house. Relieved, Mama turned abruptly on her heel, throwing a command over her shoulder: "Come on, Rosa." I was to help her look for the key, and my sisters knew she meant for them to stay with our belongings.

Mama found the key under a clay pot that held some dried-out dirt and the remains of a weedy-looking plant. We went back to the others, hurrying through the patchy, gravel-ridden, over-grown grass—our yard. It wasn't too bad. While Mama was searching for the key, I had quickly inspected the backyard; there was a garage at the end of it opening to a little alleyway. I could see a rotted door propped against the structure's opening. The broken-down building appeared to be filled with a lot of useless junk, making it a good place for kids to explore.

In the middle of the sparsely furnished living room, where an old plaid sofa stood forlornly in front of a blackened fireplace, Mama paid the driver. Thankfully, he was kind enough not to expect a tip. The house had many windows, but the wooden shutters fastening from the inside made it seem dark and de-pressing. It was also musty smelling. Although far better con-structed than my grandparents' lovable shack in Mississippi, it was still a major disappointment.

Following Mama from room to room, we noted the dampness of the walls and the green-and-black slimy stuff underneath the drafty windows, with their vinyl-backed draperies blocking the daylight. We later learned that the nasty stuff was mildew. Mama turned on lights as she led us through, telling us where we were to sleep. It was a good-sized house but had just three bedrooms. Naturally the largest one was for Mama and Daddy, and we girls were to double or triple up as we had in similar situations.

Nothing negative came from Mama's lips, but nothing positive did either. She understood that Daddy had done the best he could, and for the time being had found a house which we could afford. Wisely, my sister and I didn't mutter our complaints loud enough for Mama to overhear. We knew she wouldn't appreciate it.

In the basement, though, Velma got yelled at for walking on the back of Mama's heels. It really wasn't Velma's fault; she was

probably accidentally pushed because we were huddled right behind Mama, who was opening a thick pantry door covered with
spider webs. Inside, five empty canning jars sat on a wide wooden
shelf. It was hard for me to imagine that this house might once
have held the aroma of baking apple pies. We had never been in
a basement before and were frightened of the mice we suspected
of inhabiting the dungeon-like place. A washing machine occupied one corner; this was where Mama, Bernice, and I would be
doing the family wash.

Mama's face actually brightened when she saw the kitchen. It
was sizable and had plenty of cabinet space. Underneath a red
gingham curtain, through which the mid-afternoon sun shown
brightly, was a white porcelain table and two metal chairs. In
the dining room, which had an archway opening into the living
room, was a large table and a variety of chairs, enough to seat
all of us. It was gloomy, though. The kitchen was by far the best
thing about the house, even if the pink floral wallpaper was faded
and tattered in many places.

The immediate dilemma was what to have for dinner. The
cupboards and icebox were bare, except for a bag of black-eyed
peas Mama found in a drawer. Our pots, pans, and cooking uten-
sils, shipped earlier by train, were in a big box by the back door
that led to a little porch. Daddy had been in the house only a
week or two and hadn't unpacked the boxes or bought groceries.
He hadn't had time because he was working two shifts. Also, we
arrived on a Thursday, and Daddy was due to be paid the next day.
He had spent nearly every penny he had on our bus fare.

Placing the peas on the counter, with a purposeful look Mama
opened her pocketbook and counted her money. I don't know
how much she had, but she appeared to be satisfied. She said,

"Girls, I saw a store at the corner. We'll walk down there and get something to fix with these peas." Mama's plan certainly lifted our spirits. We were getting really hungry.

The neighborhood market wasn't much different from the one we had patronized on the corner of Avenue H in Greenwood, especially in that it was overstocked and crowded. Mama told us to wait by the door while she shopped. Evone and Velma, who were close and loved to play imaginary games, had a dialogue going, as though they were characters on one of their favorite television shows. Bernice looked homesick for Mississippi and a bit angry over the whole ordeal. Mary and I counted cars, feeling like foreigners.

Soon each of us was carrying a small sack, and Mama, like a mother duck, was leading us back to our new home. She had bought two pounds of neckbones, one onion, and some seasonings to cook with the black-eyed peas. She had also purchased a bag of sugar, some cornmeal, a dozen eggs, a gallon of milk, a loaf of bread, a pound of bologna, and a box of corn flakes. In no time, the house began to come alive and was smelling delicious. When Daddy arrived at about five-thirty, the black-eyed peas were ready, along with corn bread cooked in a big cast-iron skillet. We girls swear to this day that it was the best meal we have ever eaten. And we remember the food better than we remember our joy in seeing Daddy. It was that good.

Toledo's climate was unbearably cold for unacclimated, straight-off-the-bus southern kids. Mississippi certainly didn't have freezing blizzards. Our parkas were lightweight, and we didn't have hats, gloves, or boots. We had been northerners for about a week when, one day in early November, we made our way home from

Warren Elementary School through what looked like tundra. We might as well have moved to the Arctic. Our house was about six blocks from the school. In the blizzard, we would push forward a few steps, then turn backwards against the wintry assault in our attempt to get home. With the wind blowing snow in our faces, I had grave doubts that my sisters and I would ever find our white house.

Bernice, in a blue jacket, was far ahead of Mary and me, in our red parkas. Velma, in her brown one, was a little way back. Evone, not in school yet, was safe and warm at home with Mama, which is where I wanted to be. The icy blowing wind was dreadful. Our hair was matted down, wet with snow. Our faces were frozen, our fisted hands were numb in our pockets, and our feet and legs were covered with snow up to our bare knees. I believe we would have given our souls for a devil's hot day in the middle of a cotton field.

Naturally Bernice got home first. Mary and I were the next survivors of this journey, and Velma (we were now worried and ashamed for leaving her so far behind) came in twenty minutes later. By that time she was crying hysterically. My tears had frozen on my face. Mama was mad, worried, and sorry that she and Daddy hadn't had the money to get us warmer gear before this happened. We were just glad to see her face and to get into that warm house with its gas-burning fireplace. Mama made us strip down to our underwear in front of the leaping flames.

The next day we stayed home from school. That was all right with us, as we could see from the many windows in our house that snow was everywhere and deeper than the day before. It had taken warm baths and all night long for us to thaw out. Mama made it fun for us that day we stayed home from school. It was like the times in Mississippi, when she called us in to watch *Popeye*, her favorite cartoon.

Mama made us a delightful treat — ice cream out of the second layer of snow. It was delicious. We thought she was a genius. Later that evening Daddy came home with some winter gear bought from the Salvation Army. It didn't matter to us one bit that the items were used. We were happy, and once again our longing for Mississippi was dissipated by the warmth of our big, loving family.

On Christmas Eve, Daddy played Santa Claus, eating the graham crackers and drinking the milk we left out for him. He was still working two shifts. We saw him mostly on Sundays. He was home Christmas Day, though.

Christmas morning we woke up to a box from my grandparents that was full of pecans and toys. Then we went down to Uncle Clevester's and Aunt Vernice's house for dinner. Aunt Vernice was a bit of an alcoholic, but a nice lady and good to us. A wonderful surprise was waiting under their silver Christmas tree. They had bought us a doll house, strollers, tea sets, and several games. We were smiling from ear to ear as we all sat around the table and ate a big turkey dinner. Our first Christmas in Toledo away from our grandparents was rather nice. We lived on Vermont Street for the rest of the school year.

In the summer of 1965, we moved to 651 McClinton Nunn Homes. The projects. Gunckle Elementary School was right across the street. This move was a positive step in our lives. Our family was the first to occupy the red-brick, two-story complex that consisted of four bedrooms, a bath and a half, new appliances, living room, dining room, and utility room, with a back door that led to an enclosed court. We girls were ecstatic, because we had never before had an upstairs, or a house as nice.

Bernice got the smallest room, but she didn't have to share it. She was almost a teenager. Mary and I shared a room, sleeping together in our big iron bed brought from Vermont Street, and Velma and Evone had the room across from ours. They slept in new bunk beds. Aunt Vernice had co-signed for some furniture for our brand new dwelling, a nice French Provincial living room set and a dining room suite. Our house looked fabulous, and we were proud.

Mama and Daddy were beginning to look less tense. Daddy was in love with his recently purchased, ugly green 1959 Chrysler Imperial. Bernice especially hated that car. Our family was making rapid progress. For the first time in two years, our refrigerator and cabinets were filled with food.

On Fridays, Daddy's day off from one shift, he would have lunch waiting when we came home from school in the middle of the day. Standing at the corner traffic light, we could see his green car in front of the house. With huge grins, we'd race between the crossing guards in our haste to get home.

Daddy could make the best lunches of hamburgers or ham sandwiches with potato chips. For dessert we would have glazed donuts or oatmeal cookies. We would always have some kind of fruit — bananas, apples, grapes, pears, or peaches. Daddy looked great, and he was gaining weight. After about a year, he was home every night unless he was at his weekend army reserve duty. He was trying to make up for lost time with his girls by giving us his full attention. In the evenings, he taught us and the neighborhood kids card games and how to play baseball and do the hula hoop. We were adjusting very well to our new lives.

Moving to Toledo changed Daddy's political life drastically. At first, he was so busy trying to get our family stabilized that he had no time to take in what was happening around the world and in Mississippi. He did receive a lot of letters from Uncle David, and they talked by phone about the struggle in Greenwood. But Daddy was too removed from the situation to fully perceive the impact of the progress of blacks in Greenwood.

He was, however, very impressed with Uncle David, who was also a schoolteacher. Because of my father's and grandfather's visibility in the Greenwood struggle, Uncle David, who had not previously been involved in the movement, was asked by Samuel Block in 1965 to help organize the Greenwood Voters League. Uncle David proudly accepted the baton, and later became president of this eventually powerful organization. And, nearly three decades later, proving to be a formidable politician, he was the first black to be elected to Mississippi's state senate. Our family is very proud of his achievements.

The Vietnam War was on the evening news nightly, and Walter Cronkite was Daddy's favorite newsman. Sitting around the TV set, we witnessed for the first time wounded and dead American soldiers, as well as people of Vietnamese ancestry. We discussed the controversy over the war. My father was disturbed and definitely against the war. However, he was supportive of the American soldiers who enlisted or were drafted to fight, except for one. This exception moved Daddy to write a poem.

This is America

Lieutenant Calley is a man of
war, who took orders like he
was taught, and did his job like
he ought, is the say of most
Americans.

Moving to Ohio

This is America

In his span, he crossed many a
land, to do the things that forced
his hand. Babies cried, women and
old men died beside their wives
and babies' sides, and the whole
country laughed. Nobody cared,
nobody cried.

This is America

No one knows what hell it is,
they say, to fight in a country
where there are nothing but hills.
The people are dark and the hills
are, too. Let's kill all of them, let's
get through.

This is America

There were those who tried to
cover it up, pretending it never
happened, because no one knew.
Though shameful that it was, it
was still alright, because a white
man did it to a dark man. Right or
wrong it is war, let it die my
friends, let it die. Forget the image
of the world, forget they were
human beings, think not of them
as old men, old women, and
babies. Forget they were
unarmed, forget they were

innocent civilians, perhaps did not
know how to shoot a gun. Think
not of them as people — just
Vietcongs; for if you think of them
as people, you cease being an
American.

This is America

The military rendered a just
verdict of guilt. The whole
country shouted unfair, and called
upon the President to intervene.
He did it gladly, apparently
without a thought of justice —
trying to please all, and pleasing
none. Forget the Vietcongs my
friends, kill them all, kill everyone,
though they be babies, women
and old men unarmed.

This is America

Lt. Calley is a big man today, he is
a good soldier, they say, with
twenty-two lives buried beneath
his feet. Salute the hero of
Vietnam, salute the heroes of
World War II. Praise Hitler, Stalin,
Mussolini and all of those who
were responsible for the death of
six million Jews, and those for the
death of almost a population of
Indians, and countless numbers of

blacks — then tell me is it right
that a man should go free, tell me
if this man should be praised for
killing old men, old women and
babies unarmed. Be they white,
black or Vietcongs.

This is America

I was a soldier one time myself, a
damn good soldier, and many
more like me, but I could never
be a soldier as he, because I'm a
man, a human being with feelings,
and compassion, and my brothers
are of no color.

This is Also America

My father found that life for a black man in Ohio was very different from what it had been in Mississippi. As soon as he and Mama had established residency, they went and registered to vote. My parents found, to their relief, that they were not harassed or threatened with loss of employment. In fact, it was an uneventful day. Toledo, like the rest of the country in the mid-1960s, was not without racial problems, but the challenges there were nothing compared to those for blacks in Greenwood. Ohio was full of opportunities for Daddy. In just two years, our family made more material gains than we had in twelve years in Mississippi.

For the first time in my life, I was playing with white kids. My sisters and I loved to sing all the Beatles' hits with them, and Bob Dylan's "Blowin' in the Wind." In the McClinton Nunn Homes, we were sandwiched between two white families, and we got along with them fairly well. There were no major incidents and nothing irreparable regarding racial issues. Bernice was called a "nigger" once when she got into an argument with one of the girls. Daddy talked firmly but pleasantly with the father, and Mama talked with the mother. The girl apologized, and she never slipped up again. We all continued to play together. One family had teen-agers and the other had kids around our ages, two girls and a boy.

We found that playing and going to school with white kids was no different from being around black ones. If we experienced racism in Toledo, it was so subtle that we dismissed it. Living there gave us a greatly improved outlook on race relations. Now, that doesn't mean that we weren't called "nigger" from time to time over the years; it just means that northern bigots did not intimidate us.

At Gunckle Elementary School I had my first white teacher. Mrs. Peters, my fourth-grade teacher, wore her brown-sprinkled-with-gray hair high on top of her head, with ivory head pins securing the tendrils. She was about fifty years old, and she made everyone in our class feel special — even Buddy, an obnoxious bully. Mrs. Peters always brought in treats and encouraged us to do our best. She gave us work that was interesting and challenging, and she taught each lesson with enthusiasm. Although the student body was predominantly black, there were white kids and black kids in our class, and Mrs. Peters never discriminated.

One day she asked me to help her after school. I was delighted, because she had elevated my self-esteem by telling me that I read very well and by putting me in the highest reading group. I excelled in her class and in all my subjects because of her constant positive reinforcement. When we were loading some boxes into her car, she told me an interesting story that I have never forgotten. It was about her first day at Gunckle.

Mrs. Peters had been walking up the steps carrying a box of materials with which to decorate her room when a black boy who may have been in junior high blocked her way. When she moved to pass him, he called her a "white bitch" and spat in her face. Tears came to her eyes as she told me this story. She said it had been a very humiliating and hurtful experience to have to wipe the boy's spit from her face. I didn't know what to say to her, and I guess my eyes teared up as well, because I loved her.

I felt angry at that boy; with all the white people who did deserve to be spat at, such as Martha Lamb, the deputy registrar in Greenwood, my teacher was certainly not one of them. Mrs. Peters hugged me on the way back into the building. She told me that she understood why black people were angry at whites, especially in the South. She said that a lot of wrongs had been done to my people, and that great men like the Reverend Martin Luther King, Jr., were only standing up for what was right.

I then told her what had happened to my father in Greenwood and how he had lost his teaching job. She said she was very sorry, then assured me that things would change for the better, because blacks and whites across the United States were working together to end racism and discrimination. She said she was concerned about the riots in Detroit and Chicago; she felt that black people had justifiably lost patience with America. She explained that the black boy who spat in her face didn't know her, and he hated her only because of the color of her skin. She then told me that was not right, either. I nodded my head in agreement. I was only about ten years old, but I understood completely what she was saying to me.

During that Christmas season, my second in Toledo, Mrs. Peters brought gifts to our class. To each of us she presented a water toy; when we shook them, snow would fall gently over a Christmas scene. I had never seen anything like it. Each boy and girl also got a big candy cane. Our class felt very special as we opened our individually wrapped packages. She sat at her desk and smiled lovingly at us. You could see in her face how much pleasure she got from this kind of giving, which was truly from her heart.

In June, I helped Mrs. Peters clean up the room for summer break. Again I carried a box and walked her to her car. She gave me a kiss on the cheek and told me I had been her favorite student. I walked home alone with tears streaming down my face. I was going to miss her terribly. Aside from my father, Mrs. Peters is my favorite among the teachers I have had.

In the fall of 1966, Daddy got a teaching position at Spencer Sharples High School. He was beaming with pride when he announced the news to our family. Now Daddy was a schoolteacher again and would be for the rest of his life.

I don't want to pick cotton all my life like my parents. I have always wanted to become a schoolteacher. I want to help other boys and girls like myself. I want to prove myself to my parents, and all who have deprived me, and those who have helped me as well.

Daddy was just as much a teacher at home as he was at school, and he was constantly buying or bringing home educational games and books. Often around the dining room table he would give us math quizzes or pull out the flash cards of multiplication tables or set up spelling bees. And Daddy gave us lessons in black history long before anything of substance about black people was taught in schools. Who was called Moses? Who was Paul Laurence Dunbar? Who was Frederick Douglass? Who was Denmark Vesey? Who was Nat Turner? Who was Mary McLeod Bethune? Where is the Nile?

On and on Daddy would question us, having provided literature in which we could read about black people and about Africa. Daddy said it was important for us to know our history, and it might not be taught to us in school. He was right; I learned more about black history from my father than from anyone else. However, at the time I was more interested in what was on TV and in singing along with Marvin Gaye, Diana Ross and the Supremes, or the Jackson Five than I was in sitting around the table being quizzed by Daddy.

Daddy recounted many stories of his days as a boy growing up in Mississippi. Mama shared a lot, too, especially late in the evenings during school breaks or holidays. I remember being amused when Daddy told us that his hair had grown so long before he started school that his mother had had to braid it into two plaits like a girl's. Mama told stories about putting pestering colored boys in a headlock and about how she and Uncle William would go into town on Saturdays and hang around on Johnson Street. That was an enriching time with my parents. Their stories provided a window through which my sisters and I could peer into the past, even while we were impatient to grow up ourselves.

Some of the best conversations I had with my father occurred while I was handing tools to him as he tinkered with his beloved Chrysler Imperial. That car, "the green monster," as Bernice often referred to it, occupied space in our driveway for nearly ten years, because Daddy couldn't bear to part with it. To me it represented our talking place, where I could come as close as possible to being the son he never had. Finally, one day, Mama called the tow truck, and the "green monster" left our family for a new residence, the junkyard. But Daddy was always fixing something, and I was always there to "help."

Daddy was a teacher for the Toledo Board of Education for twenty-five years. Including the time in Mississippi, he taught for twenty-nine years, and nearly six thousand students went through his classes. Taking his profession seriously, he wore a suit and tie each day. Although his field was business, Daddy was known to sprinkle lessons in black history along through the typing and business math classes, especially when there were students operating on mediocre levels. He would spend a good part of a class period at the beginning of a semester telling them how he was a son of sharecroppers in the cotton fields of Mississippi. Daddy felt that through sharing his life experiences he could somehow motivate these students, so that they would value an education and not take opportunities for granted.

When students were having difficulties, he was more than willing to work with them after school. But high marks had to be earned. Daddy was very conservative about education. He would lavish with praise students who were hard workers and high achievers, and would offer to write letters of recommendation to colleges. If they weren't planning to continue their education, Daddy would pester them until they got sick and tired of hearing him ask, "What are your plans for college?" After graduation he would tell such a student, "I want to hear from you in a year, how you're doing in college." Then he would give the person our home phone number and address.

Daddy was an old-school kind of teacher, and he believed in figuratively kicking a lazy kid in the butt. He could not tolerate slackers. Students who came to love him and to value his support knew that he accepted no excuses for nonachievement. So any student calling or dropping by our home to speak to Daddy would also have to listen to his "you can do anything you put your mind to" sermon. Then they would sit at the dining room table and go over the assignment. Daddy's favorite motto was "Never say I can't; always say I can."

Over the years dozens of students came to our home to let him know what they were accomplishing. Many told him that it was his pushing them that led to who they were today. Some of those same students had resented him when they were in his class because he was so demanding, and a few would tell him this as they embraced him and thanked him for caring so much. Daddy, who might be in front of the house washing the car or shoveling snow, would chuckle, saying that they had had it in them all along. These students who stopped by were black, white, and Hispanic.

About a year and a half after my father was assigned to his teaching position at Spencer Sharples High School, our family bought a house in the country. A gray brick ranch with green trim on a half-acre lot, it was situated in the suburbs of Springfield, just a few miles outside of Toledo. We moved there in 1968, the year Martin Luther King, Jr., and Bobby Kennedy were assassinated, and shortly after Uncle Clevester died of kidney failure. Two years before, Daddy had made a trip to Greenwood, where Granddaddy Jordan had also succumbed to a kidney disease.

All of these deaths affected Daddy tremendously at a time in his life when he was finally prospering and enjoying his dreams. He stated on many occasions that the successes in our lives were due to the sacrifices of so many others. Because of his convictions, Daddy had a lot to share with his students about the civil rights struggle in Greenwood and around the country. Whenever he had an opportunity he would relate stories of his struggles and his triumphs as a black man in the United States of America.

Mary and I graduated from Spencer Sharples High School, and I observed Daddy teaching. My fellow students thought I was a "goody-goody," but what else could I be with my father right around the corner? For several years, Daddy was also the assistant principal and the athletic director. Unlike the colored children in Mississippi, the kids at this school weren't impressed in the least that my daddy was a schoolteacher.

Spencer Sharples was one of the toughest schools in the Toledo school system, and it was a challenge for Daddy to teach these students who, during the late 1960s and early 1970s, wore huge

Afros in their attempt to emulate militant black leaders like Huey Newton and Angela Davis. They felt that blacks like Daddy who had grown up in Mississippi should have killed the white racists, instead of practicing resistance through nonviolent marches and sit-ins. They saw professional blacks as sellouts, and didn't want to be like them. These students didn't realize that people like my father had once expressed similar viewpoints to their elders, while at the same time striving to become the best that they could be. But Daddy was patient and kept up his endless sermons, and many of his students from Spencer Sharples went on to college and to successful careers.

When my mother joined the staff as a visiting teacher to help cut down on truancy, she also found it a challenge to get these students and their families to realize the importance of achieving an education. Mama worked at this part-time position for nearly nine years, and we often found her frustrated when we came home at night.

When things got stressful and Mary and I were not fitting in, Mama and Daddy felt that we should return to our neighborhood school, Springfield High, which was predominately white. Bernice had graduated from Springfield and gone on to college. Evone and Velma, who attended Spencer Sharples Junior High for just one year, returned to Springfield and were much happier and anxiety free. Mary and I pleaded to be allowed to continue riding the eight miles with Mama and Daddy to school. They relented. We became cheerleaders and got involved in several social activities. I graduated in 1974, and Mary did so a year later.

I was salutatorian of my class, and the only blot on my graduation was that I was three months pregnant. The father of my son, Ali Andrew, was James Trout, my high school sweetheart, who had graduated from Spencer Sharples the year before, also salutatorian of his class. I was profoundly embarrassed by the situation. I was a role model and felt that I had let my parents, my sisters, my teachers, and myself down. Daddy and Mama insisted that I hold my head up, go to graduation, and accept the scholarship to the University of Toledo. I truly have been blessed to have such parents.

I had been able to excell under some fine teachers at Spencer Sharples. The late Mr. B. L. Young, my math teacher, was my favorite. The small classes and the amount of individual attention were major factors in my achievement. And, of course, Daddy, as his own father had done, was constantly preaching that education was the key to success.

Daddy taught at Spencer Sharples for fourteen years. In 1980, all three schools, elementary, middle, and high, were closed due to low enrollments, and the students were transferred to other schools in the Toledo public school district. I think it was one of the best things to happen to the area, because the kids were isolated and the area was impoverished; it was a black community surrounded by two predominately white school systems. Swanton and Springfield had drawn boundary lines around the area so they wouldn't have to deal with so many black kids. Racism is what it really was all about, although most of the black community preferred it that way, too, which meant there was prejudice on both sides.

Daddy made a great many friends among his colleagues, several of them lifelong. He had much respect for Mr. Knight, the principal; occupying that position was no easy task at Spencer Sharples. Mr. Knight afforded Daddy the opportunity to develop as an educator and an administrator.

The art teacher, Mr. Tucker, also the varsity basketball coach, was another good friend of Daddy's. All through high school I had a big crush on him, and so did my best friend, Diane Williams. He helped me to discover my art talent. Larry Johns, the class valedictorian, and I were voted the best artists in the school while under his tutelage. Mr. Tucker was very popular with the students because of his easygoing demeanor. He was funny when our basketball team was losing, rolling his eyes and pounding his fist on his knees in frustration. I'm sure more than a few curse words escaped his lips in the huddles.

Another good friend of Daddy's was Mr. Shoto, the junior varsity coach and a teacher at the middle school. Mr. Shoto was quiet and soft-spoken unless the boys messed up on the court. Then he would use his deep baritone voice to back them up a couple of steps. And two Jewish teachers made Daddy's tenure at Spencer Sharples a rewarding one. Mr. Goldstein, the shop teacher, and Daddy occasionally went fishing together. Daddy and Mr. Weinberg, our history and geography teacher, enjoyed philosophical conversations about world events. These two teachers were the only people I knew who ever called Daddy "Andy." They regarded one another highly.

Daddy's closest colleague was Mr. B. L. Young. Ironically, they almost always referred to one another as "Mr. Jordan" and "Mr. Young." Sometimes Daddy would say "B. L.," but Mr. Young always referred to Daddy as "Mr. Jordan." They had a strange but close friendship.

The female teachers whom Daddy appreciated were Miss Brown, a coteacher in the business department, and Miss Culthbert, my Spanish teacher, another favorite of mine. Mrs. Wheaton, an older woman and a mother figure to Daddy, visited our home a lot over the years. She was the oldest staff member at Spencer Sharples and had been there the longest. She was practically ancient when she finally decided to retire. Mildred Guy and Mrs. Webb were other staff members about whom Daddy spoke highly.

Daddy bragged about and raved over a number of students at Spencer Sharples, but Carl Williams, a fair-skinned, slightly built, studious young man with a husky voice, was the one who came to our house the most. Carl, a college graduate, is employed in the accounting department at the Toledo Board of Education, and still visits.

Daddy was able most fully to enjoy his range as a teacher at Bowsher High School, where he taught business education from 1980 to 1991. Mama remembers how excited Daddy was about teaching at this predominately white high school, once he had gotten over his initial disappointment at the closing of Spencer Sharples.

"When Andrew taught at Bowsher, this is where he was able to get his most stimulation as a teacher," explained Mama. "The school community was much different from Spencer Sharples. In this community there were more middle-to-upper-income families, and the students who came to school were motivated to learn. There was a greater appreciation for education, so Andrew could actually spend more time teaching and less on discipline. This was the case for both black and white students." Mama said that Daddy had few problems with students at Bowsher and that he truly enjoyed teaching there. She remembered several people of whom he often spoke.

"Andrew thought highly of the principal, James Ray, and thought he ran the school very efficiently. He thought the secretary, Bernice Guy, was the nicest lady. He greatly appreciated Barbara Tucker, who was Willie Tucker's wife from Spencer Sharples, and his fellow business teachers, Nancy Taylor and Susan Gulich. Of course, Mattie Jones and Joel Weinberg, he knew them from Spencer Sharples. They were also assigned to Bowsher." Mama said there were a lot of people at Bowsher who influenced Daddy in a positive way, but it was the students who got him there every morning. Daddy absolutely loved to teach.

Until my son, Ali, was born, Daddy had been surrounded by women. He was happy with five little girls, but having teen-agers who enjoyed dating boys got his dander up more than a few times. I'm sure there were many nights, as he sat up listening for our dates to bring us home at two in the morning, when he wished he'd had five sons instead. If it hadn't been for Mama's intervention, we probably wouldn't have dated until we were in college. Daddy was a great father, but he was strict.

I gave Daddy his first grandchild. The person Ali Andrew learned to love and cherish the most in the world, besides me, was his granddaddy. They were the best of buddies, and, for the first time since his childhood, Daddy had a boy companion to fish and hunt with. He taught his grandson everything he knew, from basketball and baseball to what had happened in Greenwood during the civil rights movement. They were practically inseparable. The first time they were separated was when I left home to marry a college boyfriend, Daryl Smith, from Youngstown, Ohio. Ali was two years old when we moved from my parents' home to a duplex close to the University of Toledo, where both my husband and I were in school. But each and every Friday after school, without fail, my parents would drop by to pick up their grandson.

Ali, holding the small, green knapsack my father had given him to pack his clothes in, would look at me with forlorn eyes. He wanted me to come, too. But I was a wife and student, and, in another year, would be pregnant with his sister, Keyomah.

Daddy eventually had eight grandchildren and was crazy about them all. Joy and Jenelle are the daughters of Mary and her husband, Jeffery Strong; Velma and her ex-husband, Marlon Shockley, are the parents of Margaux and Chrystal Lee; Kitchell, Jr., and Courtney are the son and daughter of my youngest sister, Evone, and her husband, Kitchell Michell. Daddy was proud of all his daughters and was an adored grandfather. He got along well with each of his sons-in-law, although he was strongly against my marrying the man I had chosen, and he turned out to be right.

When my father taught at Bowsher, he was able to spend more time at home, which eliminated some stress from his life. Since he wasn't serving in several capacities, he could usually come home right after school. So, unless there was a meeting or a student to tutor, he was home promptly by 2:45 every afternoon.

After school Daddy would work in the yard. He loved being outdoors, and we had the best yard in the neighborhood as a result. The garden was also a perfect place for Daddy's endless stories about his boyhood, which were certain to contain a moral. He became very reflective when he worked the soil. I can remember many conversations with Daddy in the garden. That's usually where I would find him when I came home for visits, except during the winter.

On weekdays, Daddy didn't get outdoors until after *Guiding Light* went off. How he got hooked on this soap opera is a mystery to me. I imagine he must have been sitting and talking with Mama one day when she told him to hush up, so she could catch the dialogue. All I know is that for over twelve years, he rarely missed it. Eventually, we couldn't even talk to Daddy when this program was on, since he wouldn't hear a word we said. When it ended, like clockwork he was out the door to putter around the yard.

For nearly fifteen years Daddy was able to enjoy being a family man without the pressures of trying to provide for everyone. By 1984, he and Mama were considered to be upper middle class. Four of us girls were married by then as well.

"What's for dinner, 'Rella?" Daddy was known to ask almost every day, especially on holidays. Mama is a good cook and she could fix all of Daddy's favorite dishes — sweet potato pie, any kind of greens, corn bread, and crispy fried chicken. If he cooked something for himself, it was a pan of corn bread (although he could still make the best mashed potatoes in the world). When Daddy made corn bread he was certain to have a quart of buttermilk to pour over it, which he ate out of a big mixing bowl. "Mississippi food," he said, recalling it from his boyhood days. When we were kids, Mary and I would join him. The meal was good when the corn bread was piping hot out of the oven, but it certainly could cramp up your stomach.

In Daddy's later years, family always came first. He loved the holidays when we were all together. Christmas and the Fourth of July were his favorites. He would walk around with a big smile on his face, helping Mama and us get the house ready. When we were kids, Daddy's job at Christmas was to set up the tree. We got our first live tree after we bought a home. Daddy insisted on decorating the tree himself. Five girls probably meant too many hands in the way. If we didn't like Daddy's decorating, we'd sneak in and change it while something else around the house was occupying him. If he noticed anything amiss, he never commented. He knew he was in a houseful of women.

On the Fourth of July, Daddy's job was to barbecue the meat, usually ribs and chicken. The only problem was that he would invariably come close to burning the meat while he tried to do something else around the house. It was difficult for Daddy to sit down, unless he was watching *Guiding Light* or the six o'clock news. And if he reclined in the chaise on the patio, he would fall asleep, totally oblivious to the fire blazing from the grill.

"Andrew, you're burning up the ribs," Mama would always have to yell out.

"That meat's not burnt," Daddy would holler defensively towards the kitchen window, as he rushed to the grill to douse the flames with water. Mama would shake her head and mutter under her breath, "Andrew does it every time." Our spouses, the grandchildren, and we girls would laugh in agreement.

The other big days for Daddy were his birthday and Father's Day, because we would make such a fuss over him. Unfortunately, we didn't celebrate these days with parties until we were adults. But Daddy had a good fifteen years in which he was the center of our attention, and he loved it. He wouldn't busy himself too much around the house on these special days. He would sit in the den, casually but nicely dressed in slacks and an open-collar shirt (usually something we had given him the year before), waiting for us all to arrive. It was a pleasure every time to see the joy on Daddy's face when he opened his gifts. Mama and Bernice, who still lived at home, would have cooked a big dinner. I usually brought the cake. We did the same for Mama on her birthday and Mother's Day. She enjoyed the attention as well.

But it was Daddy who beamed like a pampered king. Those days made him so happy.

Over the years, my marriage and subsequent divorce took my children and me to live in other cities in Ohio. However, Ali and Key spent many weekends, holidays, and summers with my parents, and their relationships with both were very special. At twenty-three years old, Ali still believes his grandfather was the wisest man he's ever known. He adored Daddy, just as I did all my life.

In September 1990, our world was turned upside down. Daddy was suddenly becoming thinner and complaining of pain in his right side. A big eater all his life, he was now having a hard time finishing his meals. He went to a doctor whom he had been seeing for nearly fourteen years. He was examined and sent to the hospital for a series of tests. Later in the week he called the doctor's office and was told that all he had was indigestion. He was given a clean bill of health. Relieved, Daddy wrote to Aunt Viola saying that he had been sick, but that now, according to the doctor, all was well.

But something was very wrong. Apparently, the doctor had looked over the hospital test results too quickly, and had not read the suggestion of a follow-up test to determine the origin of a mass in my father's colon. By the time the error was found, it was too late. Following an operation, Daddy spent Thanksgiving in the hospital. We went back and forth visiting him. Trying to enjoy a dinner without him didn't make any sense.

Although Daddy fought hard to regain his strength, walking and drinking gallons of Mama's carrot juice, he was rapidly declining. He spent Christmas lying on the couch, trying his best to enjoy the holiday. We decorated the tree especially nicely for him. He gave orders from his sick bed on where to place each ornament. Everything was done exactly as he specified. It was Daddy's tree, and always had been.

On March 14, 1991, I looked deeply into Daddy's jaundiced and tear-filled eyes. He returned my gaze as I helplessly held his dry hands, shriveled from chemotherapy. He had always been admired for his beautiful hands, which were large with long, tapered fingers and which were good at fixing things. In our silence we were saying goodbye. I leaned over and kissed him, whispering, "Let God love you now, Daddy." Daddy knew what I was saying. He had already told Mama a few days before that he was going home. Mama pretended not to have understood, replying, "Andrew, you're already home."

Daddy had accepted that his life was coming to a close. In just five months since the diagnosis of colon cancer, the disease had taken its toll. He was only fifty-nine years old, but he looked closer to ninety-nine. At least I got to see what my father would have looked like as an old man. It was a cruel trick on Mama, though, who could not bear to release her husband of thirty-six years. It was too distressing for her to say goodbye to her lover and best friend, the father of their five daughters, the grandfather of their eight grandchildren. It was extremely difficult for all of us, because Daddy was the center of our family. He was our teacher.

Andrew L. Jordan died on March 15, 1991, just before midnight. I was in the parking lot of the hospital with my children when I felt his spirit leaving him. Looking up into the clear black sky, I knew that Daddy's struggles had ended and that he had finally triumphed.

He was very proud of his five daughters. Three of us have college degrees. I graduated from Ohio State University, majoring

in psychology, and now own a consulting and management training firm. Velma is a registered nurse. Bernice has an associate
degree in library science from the University of Toledo, and is
currently working on a business degree at Lords College. She
lives with Mama and commutes to school. Mary and her husband, Jeff, have worked for Toledo Jeep for over twenty years.
Evone, an administrative assistant, and her husband, Kitchell, an
industrial engineer, work for the same company in Michigan
where they live.

Daddy would be proud to know that his grandchildren have
valued their educations and are pursuing their goals. Ali graduated from Ohio State in under three years, majoring in political
science. After a year and a half in law school, he decided he
wanted to become an actor, and he has since been modeling and
acting. Key was the first black valedictorian at Worthington
Kilbourne High School. She is a prelaw major at Ohio State, on
a full scholarship. Joy is studying to become a nurse at Owens
Technical College. Janelle, a first-year student at the same school,
is majoring in English. Margaux, Chrystal Lee, and Kitchell, Jr.,
are in high school and doing well. Kitchell, Jr., works hard in
school and is a fine athlete and artist. The baby of the family,
Courtney, is in the fifth grade. (She has to remember Daddy
mostly from photos, since she was just three years old when he
died.) Mama is pursuing a college degree at the University of
Toledo. I know Daddy would be especially proud of her.

Regrettably, Daddy died before learning that Byron De La
Beckwith was found guilty of the murder of Medgar Evers. In
1994, a valiant and courageous white federal prosecutor, Bobby
DeLaughter, who was a kid when Medgar was assassinated, was
finally able to obtain a guilty verdict in Jackson. Myrlie Evers-
Williams was the driving force behind the reopening of the case.

For thirty years she had kept the original trial transcripts, which indicated numerous discrepancies and Beckwith's direct involvement in Evers's murder.

But, even in 1994, some white Mississippians did not see why it made sense to put an old racist in prison. "Let bygones be bygones" was a typical lament from some of his supporters. DeLaughter's efforts were met with resistance and threats. However, many whites as well as blacks were jubilant about Beckwith's finally having to pay for his crime. He had been free to walk around and brag for much too long. For Myrlie, the Evers children, Medgar's brother, and all other survivors, the victory was well worth the wait.

In the years since Daddy's death, we have tried to live each day the best we can without him. The holidays are still the hardest, because his absence is so apparent. At first I did not expect, in my sorrow, that the sun would rise or the moon would shine or the stars ever really twinkle for me again. My mother's sorrow was even deeper, almost unreachable. But, as time passes, I am healing. We are healing. And we remember Daddy, thinking of him, in heaven, being what he was here on earth — a schoolteacher.

I hope that children of all races everywhere will not assume that everything has come about solely because of one man's generosity. But rather they know that all people within a country contribute to its growth. I hope they work toward the betterment of their country and not contribute to its downfall, and that they realize that all people are brothers and sisters, and no people can live without the other for long.